HANDMADE TO SELL

HELLO CRAFT's Guide to OWNING, RUNNING, and GROWING Your Crafty Biz

by Kelly Rand

with Christine Ernest, Sara Dick, and Kimberly Dorn

Illustrations by Jaime Zollars

POTTER
CRAFT
New York

For those who want to make something awesome

Published in the United States by Potter Craft, an imprint of the Crown
Publishing Group, a division of Random House, Inc., New York.
www.pottercraft.com
www.crownpublishing.com

POTTER CRAFT and colophon are registered trademarks of Random
House, Inc.

Library of Congress Cataloging-in-Publication Data
Handmade to sell : Hello Craft's guide to owning, running, and growing your
crafty biz / by Kelly Rand ; with Christine Ernest . . . [et al.] ; illustrations by
Jaime Zollars — 1 [edition].
p. cm.

Includes index.

1. Selling—Handicraft. 2. Handicraft—Marketing.
3. Small business—Management.

HF5439.H27 R37 2012

2011046776

ISBN 978-0-307-58710-7
eISBN 978-0-307-58711-4

Printed in the United States of America

Photography credits: pages 65, 66, courtesy Shauna Alterio; page 67,
courtesy Rhonda Wyman, Figs + Ginger; pages 70, 71, courtesy Charm City
Craft Mafia; pages 106 (top), 108 (bottom), courtesy Tasha McKelvey; page
106 (bottom), courtesy Jordan Perme, Horrible Adorable; pages 107, 108
(top), 109–111, courtesy Hello Craft

Book design by Jenny Kraemer
Illustrations by Jaime Zollars
Cover design by Jenny Kraemer
Cover illustration by Jaime Zollars

10 9 8 7 6 5 4 3 2 1

First Edition

ACKNOWLEDGMENTS

Hello Craft was born one evening at a restaurant, over much laughter. Many thanks go to Tina Seamonster for being there at the beginning and for her continued support as a member of Hello Craft's board of directors. Hello Craft wouldn't be what it is without Tina and the other wonderful and dedicated members of our board. Thank you.

Much thanks to Kate McKean for her tireless support, enthusiasm, and meaningful advice. Also, thank you to our editors and all the wonderful people at Potter Craft.

And, most important, thank you to our dear friends and families, who helped see us through the process of writing this book. Much love and gratitude.

Now go make something awesome.

CONTENTS.

CHAPTER 5

Selling Online

CHAPTER 6

Selling at Craft Fairs

CHAPTER 7

Talking Shop

CHAPTER 8

Marketing

CHAPTER 9

Expanding Your Business

CHAPTER 10

Walking the Walk

A LETTER OF
WELCOME

Hello! We're so excited to have you here! We four crafters and craft fair organizers share a love of making, and we hope you'll find this book to be chock full of useful information on how you can start, grow, and sustain your awesome crafty business. Having been involved in the handmade community for, well, basically for our whole lives, as well as having taken part in the founding of Crafty Bastards Arts & Crafts Fair, we know that this handmade thing is a big deal.

Hello Craft, formed in 2008, is a 501(c)6 nonprofit trade association dedicated to the advancement of independent crafters and the handmade movement as well as to empowering small-business owners and educating the public on the benefits of buying handmade. These basic tenets are all meant to support the handmade community and to reinforce one another. We provide accessible crafting opportunities by bringing our Make Something

Awesome Area to various events around the country, bringing together crafters who want to share their love of making with the public, who are given the opportunity to try different craft projects and learn the joys of making.

Hello Craft also highlights the benefits of buying handmade by producing indie craft markets such as Crafty Bastards Arts & Crafts Fair and the Show of Awesome. These markets help support the members of the handmade community and provide unique shopping environments where consumers can purchase handmade goods and interact directly with the makers.

The biggest focus of Hello Craft is the advancement of independent makers and the empowerment of small-business owners. Everyone seems to be clamoring for the secrets of success for starting and growing a crafty business. DIYers want to make and sell, and consumers want unique and personal products—not the same mass-produced things everyone else has. Hello Craft aims to bring makers and consumers together.

There hasn't been a whole lot of business information out there that speaks to crafters. Sure, there are the Small Business Administration and the Chamber of Commerce, but are you asleep yet? We know that crafters are different. We're DIY to the core, and no amount of Charlie Brown teacher-speak is gonna make it through. But you know what? We could all use a dose of sound business advice. For that reason, Hello Craft produced the very first Summit of Awesome in Washington, DC, in 2009. This three-day conference is aimed at empowering crafters to become small-business owners and to teach the joys of making. Successful crafty folks came to talk about their experiences. Sessions ranged from a seminar on product development to one titled "The Ins and Outs of Wholesale." The second annual Summit of Awesome took place in Portland, Oregon, and the third in Baltimore, Maryland, and each time the summit improved, getting more awesome from year to year. Because crafters are the presenters, it all makes sense to the crafters who attend.

With the continued success of the Summit of Awesome and with more and more people looking for crafty business information, the next logical step was for

us to boil down the summit into portable book form. So here it is: the Summit of Awesome in paperback. From this book, you'll learn from crafty pioneers who have come before. And it's all in language you can understand. We're bringing the crafty business knowledge to the people. (Or at least to the people who buy this book!)

We are *your* people. We get that you want to learn and make on your own. We know you are DIY, and so this book caters especially to you. We're here to guide you, be your personal cheerleaders, give you that "kick in the pants" you might need, and tell you that while you can do this, it is going to be *hard work*. You *can* do it, though—and you can be amazingly awesome at the same time.

We love you!
xoxo,
Kelly, Christine, Sara, and Kim

Chapter

1

"Are you all right?"

"Yes. I need to be on my own. Please go away."

"Has something happened?"

He begins to shudder all over, as if he's had ice water poured over him. "The police called me earlier. I went into the station. They said they had news. I can't believe it—they told me weeks ago when I gave them our list that they'd checked on him and they hadn't. They've only just found out."

I can't approach him. Instinctively, I know if I touch him, if he has to turn, he won't be able to get these words out. I wait silently.

"Tyler's out. He'd been moved to an open prison for exemplary behavior, and he went missing. He's been out on the run for a year, and I didn't know. I never knew. I gave the police his name, and they didn't check until now and they've put us in more danger. It's in their files. How can they have messed this up?"

And so the shadow man has a name. And a motive.

"They can't protect us," Dan says. "They couldn't even check on him properly when all this time, he's been on the loose." He leans his head against the window. "It's my fault, it's my fault, it's my fault—"

"Dan—"

"Get out. Please get out. I can't deal with you right now. Just please get out!" And he crashes his fist against the wall.

I hurry out of the study and close the door. I can hear the sound of my husband sobbing through the door. My blood is frozen in my veins.

53

DAN IS GONE WHEN PORTIA and I get up in the morning. I check the study cautiously in case he's still in there, but there's nothing except a half-full mug of cold coffee on his desk. Once office hours have started, I call the police station. Booth isn't available—on annual leave, they tell me—but I press the issue. I'm transferred to another detective.

"I need to know what's going on. Why weren't we told until yesterday that Anthony Tyler was out of prison? How can you make a mistake like this? My daughter died!"

"There's no evidence to suspect Tyler at the present time, Mrs. Fulton," is the smooth reply.

"That might be true, Detective, but if you'd been on the receiving end of police suspicion as I have, maybe you'd be a little more understanding of how angry I am that someone who does have an actual motive is out there and nobody told us!"

I hang up. I'm too angry to deal with them right now.

Instead, I need to do something practical. The police may be incapable of protecting us, so I need to equip myself. I don't even know what this man looks like, so I go online and search for details of that old case. Sure enough, I find a police mug shot in the newspaper report.

He's in his mid-thirties with a smooth-looking face and high cheek-bones. He's moderately good-looking, with nothing exceptional about his appearance at all, other than his eyes. They look too detached to be human, or is that my imagination because I know what he did?

MAKING
THINGS

I n the spring of 2011, *Extreme Craft* blogger Garth Johnson attended the San Francisco Fine Art Fair. The show filled the Festival Pavilion at the Fort Mason Center with fine-art gallery booths offering works in postwar and contemporary art. He had a pleasant enough time. The economy was slowly coming back after being hit hard a couple years before, and Garth thought to himself, "Okay, this is nice. People are buying all of this fine art."

Then Garth made his way over to the San Mateo Event Center for a much less traditional event, Maker Faire, which was held the same weekend. Maker Faire describes itself as "the World's Largest DIY Festival." More than 90,000 people attended this two-day showcase of innovation, creativity, and DIY culture. Garth says, "I felt all this energy and people making things themselves and being curious about how things are made."

It is a simple and powerful idea that we, as humans, are born with the need to create. And chances are you have been creating for a long time. Whether you like to cook, sew, print, or design, it's all *making*.

There's a certain feeling crafters get when they pick up the tools of their trade. When you put your creative ideas into motion—firing up your sewing machine, burning a silk screen, or adding a "made by" tag to your plush figure—it's amazing.

> ## *All of us are makers.*
>
> —**DALE DOUGHERTY,** founder and CEO
> of *Make* magazine and Maker Faire,
> TED Talk, January 2011

You use your hands to make. What a simple yet profound statement. Using your hands to create physical objects, you're building a connection with the things you make. You are personally involved, and there's an intimate tie between you and these objects. Your blood, sweat, tears, and emotions have been knit, stitched, drawn, and soldered into every single detail.

So why do we make? Everyone makes for his or her own personal reasons, but the need to create is ingrained in us. "I think the human brain is absolutely wired to be able to take things apart and reassemble them in different ways," Garth explains. Makers have a curiosity, and a need to touch, and a desire to get their hands dirty.

Learning how to do it yourself is accessible to everybody. Anyone can make something. The do-it-yourself mentality is attracted to challenges. It's empowering to learn a new skill and to continue to perfect it. And there's a profound sense of achievement in the completion of a project—a quiet celebration of the limitless possibilities of craft.

Making things by hand also produces a meditative state. Whether you're knitting, sewing, throwing a pot, drawing, screen-printing, or what have you, you'll hit the sweet spot and get "in the zone." Your mind will find a quiet place and be at peace.

By buying into the DIY movement, crafters are stating their desire to live a life full of curiosity, learning, and doing. Makers relish the control they have over the creation of objects. Handmade gives you complete control of the entire creative process, and this control spills over into a sense of pride in and ownership of your life. As Faythe Levine says in her foreword to Jo Waterhouse's *Indie Craft*: "Craft can change lives. Art can heal. Making with your hands is empowering."

The Handmade Movement

Creating and making with one's own hands is not a new idea, and neither is the concept of being crafty. These ideas have been around a very long time, but in the past ten to fifteen years there has been a resurgence of interest in creating by hand. Once again, it's in vogue.

Traditional crafting skills such as sewing, knitting, and quilting started to pop up all over North America, Britain, and Australia in the 1990s. The new crafters weren't doing crocheted doilies and knitted washcloths, however. The craft coming out of the late '90s and early 2000s was a different kind of craft. It was traditional, but with a twist. Craftster.org, an online forum where crafters share their creations, sums up the new aesthetic with its tagline, "No tea cozies without irony."

That attitude arose from the punk culture of the early 1990s. The emerging generation of crafters grew up with this ironic punk sensibility and brought it with them when they embraced the DIY ethos. They took traditional materials and techniques and made them contemporary and relevant to the times. As Faythe Levine explains, "Our community was changing the way that people ingest creativity, making it approachable and pushing the boundaries. We took craft to the street, reshaping a word that has and will continue to have many definitions."

Roots in Rebellion

While there is no one reason behind the resurgence of DIY culture, we can understand it better by exploring a few themes that infuse the current handmade movement.

Interest in arts and crafts is cyclical. It has a generational component. First came the Arts and Crafts Movement in England

and the United States. That began in the mid-nineteenth century and extended into the early decades of the twentieth century. Then, as Garth Johnson explains, "twenty or thirty years later there was a postwar craft movement with the Black Mountain School. Then there was a counterculture wave in the late '60s, and we are absolutely ripe for another wave of craft, another generation discovering craft on their own." We are now experiencing that wave.

Just as examples of how ubiquitous crafting and the handmade industry have become, there are now more than 400,000 shops on the online marketplace Etsy, and Ravelry, an online knitting and crochet community, has 2 million users.

While these are very mainstream numbers, the current popularity of craft also has a basis in rebellion. Most of the people in the generation that's getting interested and involved in the handmade movement right now probably weren't taught how to sew, cook, or make anything by hand while growing up. As Garth explains, becoming a DIYer is "a way to raise your middle finger to your parents and your upbringing and say, 'Look, screw you. I'm going to rebel and learn to embroider and pickle things.'"

A Backlash Against Technology

Technology has revolutionized our world in a very short time. Even though many technological advances make things easier in our day-to-day lives, they also take us farther away from making things from scratch. This generation's handmade movement might have originated, in part, in a backlash against technology.

The resurgence of making has kept pace with the rise of technology. Interestingly, there's a push-pull relationship between the two, in that the current handmade movement takes advantage of all that technology has to offer while at the same time worshiping objects created by hand. The handmade community may in some sense be "against" technology, but that technology has also helped create the handmade community. Crafters have taken something impersonal—computer technology—and turned it into a highly effective tool for communication and production. DIY culture and community have developed on the Internet: not only is there a great deal of how-to information from old books and magazines readily available online but the Internet has also helped build a community of makers, facilitating connections regardless of location. Through numerous online resources, crafters are networking, sharing, and learning from one another via tutorials, video how-to's, blog posts, and social media updates.

A New Feminist Perspective

Looking around the handmade room, you'll see an overwhelming number of women at the crafting table. Many, many women have been inspired to try their hands at long-dormant crafts—even some that used to be thought constraining from a feminist perspective. They've been learning skills that their mothers had rejected in their youth, when fiber- and textile-based crafts were viewed as something that women did as a domestic pastime or hobby.

But part of the indie craft scene involves reclaiming those crafts and redefining what counts as "feminist." While women seem to dominate the indie craft field, their work is not domestic in nature, nor is it stereotypically "feminine." The subject matter is very different from that of traditional crafts. And, besides, there are now lots of crafty men out there doing the same kinds of crafts! As Greg Der Ananian, founder of the Bazaar Bizarre craft fairs, says on bazaarbizarre.org, "Crafts have long been denigrated as a feminized form of expression, but Bazaar Bizarre represents an impulse to revalue the abilities our mothers and grandmothers taught us, while making them our own. It's as much about tradition as it is about change."

Quality-of-Life Consumerism

In Jo Waterhouse's book *Indie Craft,* Magda Sayeg, the mother of "yarn bombing" with Knitta Please, explains that she's part of the handmade movement because it "emphasizes handmade artistry as a reaction to the mass-produced culture we're immersed in." As Waterhouse continues, "If you make handmade items, whether for practical reasons (clothing or home wares), for decorative reasons, or as gifts, you are turning your back on the mass-produced items found on most high streets or in

shopping malls. You are creating something unique, personal and special."

We all want a good quality of life, and handmade is a reaction against mass-produced cookie-cutter culture in favor of a more personal and unique consumer model. With the rise of robotic assembly lines, people became less connected to how things are actually made. We lost the *context* of the objects in our lives. Handcrafted items were devalued, and people lost some time-honored skills, like how to sew, how to grow a garden, and how to can vegetables. But reclaiming these skills creates a sense of pride. There's a sense of accomplishment when you know how to be a maker. We need these skills. We need a curiosity about how things are made. The handmade movement has sparked that curiosity, and we're seeing the re-creation of the context once again.

Consumers were told that big-box stores were the norm. You go and you buy and you don't really know where the products are coming from or how they are made. Not only that, but there is a loss of individuality when everyone buys the same shirt. This was expected and tolerated. But then the handmade movement came along and created a backlash against this cold consumer model. People started wanting more connections with their objects and with the people who made them—an experience they couldn't find in a big-box store.

Fulfilling Work

Handmade is the next iteration of the American Dream. Working in a handmade career, you set your own hours and your own expectations for success. You're not just another cog in the wheel of some large corporation. It's about being your own boss and driving your own success, in whatever form you want that to take.

Making for a living lets you pursue a life that's *worth* living. You have the opportunity to shape that life, to climb to a place where you're able to survive and make a decent wage while also being comfortable with what you're doing. No one gets into the handmade business world to make billions of dollars, and you shouldn't think you will. It is a niche market that is very small. But small can be sustainable. How you go about achieving this is up to you—and something the rest of this book will help teach you.

The Craft Organization Development Association (CODA) estimates

5 MILLION

American makers sell their crafts.

History of Contemporary Craft

It's good to take a look back and know you are standing on the shoulders of the many talented and amazing makers who have come before you. This timeline shows how the contemporary handmade movement and industry has evolved since the early 1990s.

As the movement continues to develop, changes continue to happen—for instance, the demise of *ReadyMade* magazine in 2011. The good news is that, despite such a loss, the handmade community is still going strong. In 2011, Crafty Bastards Arts & Crafts Fair recorded more than 30,000 attendees to its one-day show. In 2011, Maker Faire had a record year, with 90,000 attendees. Etsy now has more than 400,000 sellers, and Ravelry boasts more than 2 million users.

Where the movement goes next is up to you. How will you help to shape it? Only time will tell.

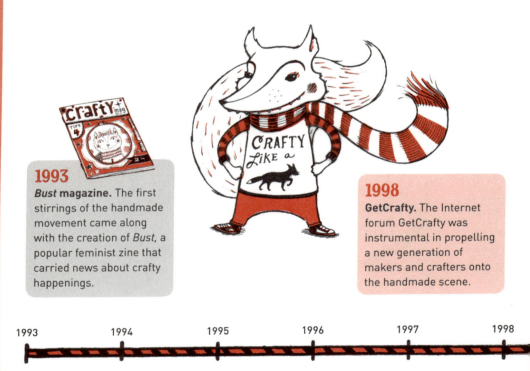

1993
Bust **magazine.** The first stirrings of the handmade movement came along with the creation of *Bust,* a popular feminist zine that carried news about crafty happenings.

1998
GetCrafty. The Internet forum GetCrafty was instrumental in propelling a new generation of makers and crafters onto the handmade scene.

1993   1994   1995   1996   1997   1998

1999

Buyolympia. The Buyolympia website pioneered online selling for indie artists and crafters.

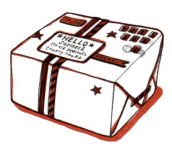

2000

Stitch 'n Bitch. This modern take on knitting circles helped make this once-antiquated craft cool again.

2001

Bazaar Bizarre. The handmade movement really picked up steam with the creation of Bazaar Bizarre, which according to founder Greg Der Ananian "began in the Boston area as a hodgepodge of friends and acquaintances cobbling together their handcrafted DIY wares to sell and staging an offbeat entertainment extravaganza." This quintessential indie craft fair expanded to Los Angeles and Cleveland in 2004.

2002

ReadyMade magazine. This DIY magazine helped inspire a generation to get their hands dirty and make something. Featuring DIY projects, *ReadyMade* offered a glimpse into the handmade lifestyle, showcasing creative jobs in the column "How'd You Get That Fucking Awesome Job?" (HYGTFAJ) and encouraging creative reuse with each issue's MacGyver contest.

2003

Craft Mafia. Started in Austin, Texas, by nine crafty businesswomen, Craft Mafias have spread across the United States as craft collective and business support groups to help foster creative indie businesses.

Craftster. With the Craftster forum, the Internet continued to open up the crafty world and connect devoted members of the handmade community by allowing people to share their creations.

Renegade Handmade. The Renegade Handmade fair got its start in Chicago in the fall of 2003; expanded to Brooklyn, New York (in the McCarren Park Pool, in Greenpoint), in 2005; and then set up in San Francisco in 2008, Los Angeles in 2009, and Austin in 2010. In 2011, Renegade Handmade jumped across the pond, hosting its first international fair in London, England.

(continues)

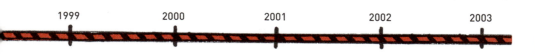

1999   2000   2001   2002   2003

2004

***Bust* Craftacular.** *Bust* jumped into the craft fair circuit with the *Bust* Magazine Craftacular in 2004. This juried craft fair was a natural extension for the zine (now magazine) that has always supported handmade and the DIY movement.

Crafty Bastards Arts & Crafts Fair. The first Crafty Bastards Arts & Crafts Fair opened up the handmade economy to the Mid-Atlantic region, revealing an indie edge to the often straitlaced city of Washington, DC.

Magpie. Annual craft fairs were soon joined by year-round brick-and-mortar shops showcasing the same handmade goods one can find on the craft fair circuit. Opening in Somerville, Massachusetts, in 2004, Magpie, a leader in this arena, was founded by some of the same folks responsible for Bazaar Bizarre.

2005

Big Cartel. Giving bands the ability to sell their merchandise online was the original idea behind Big Cartel. This online shopping cart has since grown in appeal and now handles online sales for some 100,000 creative independent businesses.

Etsy. The online handmade world was no longer limited to forums, message boards, and LiveJournal entries after Etsy burst onto the scene in 2005, making it easy for any handmade business to set up shop online. Today, Etsy has become synonymous with handmade.

***Make* magazine.** This print magazine caters to those interested in science and technology. *Make* encourages people to have a better understanding of how things are made, offering DIY projects and amateur science experiments.

2006

Maker Faire. Not just crafters but makers of many kinds were captivated by Maker Faire, which opened in San Mateo, California, in 2006, bringing Bazaar Bizarre with it. The fair brought backyard makers and basement tinkerers together to show off their amazing creations.

2004   2005   2006

2007

Craft magazine. The first issue of *Make*'s sister magazine, *Craft,* hit newsstands in 2007, showcasing DIY craft projects and articles about the handmade community. *Craft* ceased print publication within a year of launch, however, and now lives online as a blog.

Craft Congress. The first Craft Congress took place in 2007 and brought together industry leaders to talk shop and share their vision for the future of crafting.

Renegade Handmade storefront. In 2007, Renegade put down roots as a brick-and-mortar, opening the doors to its permanent retail store in Chicago, Illinois.

Ravelry. Part social network, part pattern placeholder, Ravelry caters to the knitting and crochet community, offering a place to crowd-source patterns and support an offline community.

2008

ArtFire. Another online marketplace for crafters, ArtFire is driven by community. It tailors its features and functions to users' input and does its best to help sellers sell globally.

Hello Craft. Capitalizing on crafters' need for more business information, Hello Craft formed its trade association in 2008 to support the handmade community and indie businesses.

2009

Land. Buyolympia expanded its business by opening a retail shop and gallery, Land, in front of its warehouse in Portland, Oregon. Land is a natural extension of Buyolympia's successful online business of selling the wares of independent artists and crafters.

Summit of Awesome. Hello Craft launched its business conference for crafters, the Summit of Awesome, in 2009 with the aim of bringing seasoned and novice crafty business owners together to learn and make.

2010

I Heart Art. Etsy began forming its I Heart Art chapters to partner with colleges and museums to provide educational resources and offline support to creative communities. The Portland, Oregon, chapter was formed in 2010, and the Baltimore and San Francisco chapters in 2011.

2007　　　2008　　　2009　　　2010

Chapter

2

STARTING YOUR
CRAFTY BIZ

- -

C onsider what place you want making to have in your life. Do you want a hobby or a business? Chances are that if you're reading this book, you want a business. But take note: If you want a successful business but can only dedicate the amount of time and attention you would to a hobby, your business will be less than successful and your self-esteem will tank.

That doesn't mean you should stop yourself from starting simply because you don't have it all figured out at the moment. More than one successful crafter out there has at one time or another admitted, "I don't know what I'm doing!"

Be honest with yourself about what you want out of your craft business. If you're looking for an easy buck, this isn't the path for you. You need a lot of drive and cannot be afraid of hard work, or of failure. Rhonda Wyman, who runs a jewelry and stationery business called Figs & Ginger, along with her husband, Elijah, based in Asheville, North Carolina, puts it this way: "I believe that people think it's easier than it looks, and I don't think they realize all the work that must go into it. You can't stop working, and there is no one to cover your shift. You have to be prepared for the work. It isn't a nine-to-five job. It's more like a nine-to-midnight type of job."

Successful crafters are not necessarily born with special talent; many just have an unending drive to do whatever it takes to succeed. Crafters who decide to make a living with their art have a lot of ambition and a thirst for knowledge. They are highly entrepreneurial, not afraid to try new things, and, most important, not afraid to fail. They are not afraid of hard work, or of working long hours. When you're your own boss, you have to throw out the idea of a nine-to-five job. (But most crafters who decide to give it a go never wanted a nine-to-five to begin with!)

The Small Business Administration estimates that there are 27.2 million small businesses in the United States. More than half of working Americans either own or work for a small business. So if you decide to start a crafty business, you will be among good company.

Why Do You Make?

Is your making going to remain a hobby? Or could you turn what you do for fun and stress relief into a business? Here is a quick breakdown of the differences between being a hobbyist and a businessperson:

Hobbyist	Businessperson
You create in your spare time.	You create and plan all the time.
You make primarily for yourself or friends and family.	You make primarily to sell to strangers.
You give away your creations.	You can't afford to give away too many of your creations.
You make for stress relief.	Making can be a major stress.
You make to have a creative outlet.	You don't have as much of a creative outlet.
You occasionally sell an item for fun and, possibly, extra cash.	You are selling year round.
You cannot deduct materials, trainings, and supplies from your taxes.	You can deduct materials, trainings, and supplies from your taxes.

Eyes Wide Open

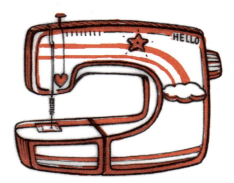

No matter how rewarding it turns out to be, starting a business is hard work. It takes time. A lot of time. It also takes dedication and, most important, passion. You also need a tough skin. Although the handmade community is generally a loving and welcoming one, you'll be taking the results of all your blood, sweat, and tears and turning them over to a public that can be very cruel. The Internet can be particularly cruel because of its anonymity. It's important to remember that while your family and close friends may think your creations are beautiful and wonderful and encourage you to sell your wares, there may be a big difference between what an insular circle thinks and how the general public responds.

Don't get us wrong: We're not saying that you shouldn't turn your hobby into a business—after all, that's what this book is all about! But how you go about doing it makes all the difference. Starting slowly, building a customer base, refining your products and brand, and learning from your process are business gold. Learning from others' mistakes and utilizing all the crafty resources the community has to offer are vital. Turning your hobby into a business won't happen overnight, and it may take years before it starts feeling like a "real" business to you. You need to have reasonable expectations and set your course for smart growth.

As Etsy founder and former CEO Rob Kalin said in an interview with *Inc.* magazine in 2011: "There's this really interesting shift that happens when you're running an Etsy business, where you have to change your approach from 'I make clothing' to 'I'm making a living making a business that makes clothing.' A lot of people either can't or don't want to make the shift, because it means seeing things in a different light." This is largely true, and at some point you will need to make a fundamental shift regarding your business. For one thing, you'll be spending more of your time on administration and less on creating and making, which probably got you into this field in the first place.

Don't Quit Your Day Job—Yet

When you start to market your craft, it is best to start slow. See how your knitted drink cozies or bird jewelry do at a local market. Sell to a friend of a friend who is looking for a gift, and then grow and plan from there. When you are at the point where you're rushing out the door of your day job at 5:00 p.m. to go home and sit in front of your sewing machine, or when you're using up all your weekend time selling at local markets, or when you're finding that you have to say no to new and bigger opportunities because your day-job obligations won't allow you to pursue them, it may be time to consider making the jump to being a full-time crafter.

This tipping point will be different for everyone. But how do you know when's the right time for you? When Rebecca Pearcy started Queen Bee Creations out of a corner of her bedroom fifteen years ago, she had two part-time jobs and was sewing on the side. As she tells it, "I just at some point decided that if I was going to ever find out if I was going to be successful, I needed to put full-time into it. So I quit both of my part-time jobs and put all of my efforts into my little business, and that sort of was like the point of no return."

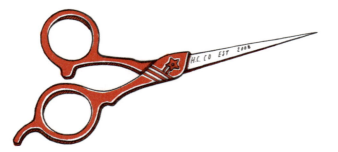

Business Formation

When you start to sell either crafty goods (your products) or services (for example, advertisements on your blog), you are essentially running a business. You need to start to think of yourself as such and need to consider the legal ramifications of operating the business. You need to consider how to protect yourself, your products, and your money. You don't want to open yourself up to additional taxes and fines—or even a lawsuit—because you are not a legally formed business.

The first step is to officially organize your crafting operations as a business entity. This means registering with the government and paying taxes in accordance with the kind of business you set up. There are several different ways you can form your crafty business; the different kinds of entities are taxed at different rates and offer different levels of legal protection for you, your business, and your money.

Be sure to research the specific laws of your state so you are in compliance. The easiest way to do this is to check out the information available on the website of your state's secretary of state or Department of State. You'll also want to check with your city's government, as you may be required to have a municipal business license to run your crafty business.

The Smart Way to Make the Jump to Full-Time
An Interview with Becky Striepe

Becky Striepe, who runs her Glue and Glitter online shop from her Atlanta, Georgia, home, began making in 2005. She started out with jewelry, but she quickly grew to hate all the waste she was creating. Her heart just wasn't in it. So she switched to making her now-signature eco-friendly lunch bags after a friend taught her how to sew. Learning this new skill awakened her crafty spirit, as it was so easy to get reclaimed and organic fabric to work with.

Becky's crafting went from a hobby to a part-time job when she switched to sewing. That was partly because it's easier to fill up a booth with fabric products than with jewelry, but it's also because she had truly found her heart. She branched out, selling her eco-friendly lunch bags and an expanding product line—including her thrifted-fabric "cupcaprons" (aprons with eco-felt cupcake pockets) and pillows—at a few more festivals and neighborhood fairs. She opened an Etsy shop, got involved with a local craft group, and started blogging about environmental issues. Her business was growing. People started to recognize her and her brand from her participation in the neighborhood festivals, and this helped to grow her customer base.

Because she couldn't take credit cards at the fairs, Becky's Etsy shop provided a back-stop for potential lost sales. Customers who wanted to use credit cards to buy her items were able to go to her Etsy shop, where they had that option.

Soon, Becky reached the point where she was working a forty-hour-a-week day job, then coming home and sewing to keep up with the demand for her lunch bags and writing to fulfill her blogging obligations. A free night was rare. It was getting to be too much, and she needed to find a better balance.

Q: **How were you able to quit your full-time job?**

A: My plan was to save for two months, after which I thought I could just figure it out, but my husband quickly squished that idea. So we sat down and worked out a one-year savings plan. It was very aggressive. We figured out our monthly budget for the mortgage, utilities, phone, cell phones, cable, and so on, and then figured out, ideally, what was my half of the responsibility for a year. We also added in a year's worth of craft supplies and market/fair expenses. That total was our savings goal.

We then started the very aggressive plan we'd set out, and when we hit the end of the year, I put in my two weeks' notice. It was intense, but totally worth it. It was nice to know that even if no one bought a "cupcapron," we would be okay.

Q: **What are some of the things that happened that you weren't expecting?**

A: Setting up my business legally was a huge learning experience, and I wasn't ready for some of the expenses within that process—such as my business license. But luckily they weren't enormous.

I was also surprised at how helpful the city and the state and even the IRS were about setting up my business, and not scary at all. I started by calling one agency, which connected me to others. Each time I was very up front about not knowing what I was doing.

Q: **What are some of the lessons you've learned from this process?**

A: Once you are full-time and paying taxes on your business, you have to raise your prices to make a living wage. I've become more choosey about which shows and fairs I apply to now. The customers at the bigger shows get handmade and understand why things cost what they do, but at smaller neighborhood shows, people are looking for bargains. It's hard to offer those prices and keep the lights on at the same time.

It also helps to have a business plan even if it is super loose. My husband made me make one, and I am so glad. I also created a spreadsheet that lists all my products and shows total net income for a year. It lets me see different ways to focus my business. I can see what the total would look like if I sold more lunch bags or "cupcaprons." I highly recommend talking to a good accountant. They can tell you how to do your books so that tax time is not a nightmare.

Q: **Do you think you made the right decision in moving to full-time crafting?**

A: Absolutely! I've never been this broke since college, but I have never been this happy, either. I get up in the morning and get to work on things I want to work on all day. It is all for something that I care about. My heart's in it.

Sole Proprietorship

The easiest way to set up your business—and one that's quite popular among crafters, especially those who are just starting out—is as a sole proprietorship. In fact, there are between 15 and 20 million small businesses in the United States that are sole proprietorships. A sole proprietorship means there is only one owner of the business and you, the owner, receive all the profit.

The only form you may have to file is a business-name registration. If you choose to do business under a name that is not your given name, you may need to register it with your state. Because this is basically the only form required for registration, it costs little to nothing to set up a sole proprietorship. You'll be claiming your business's income and expenses on your personal tax return, as your business is essentially an extension of you. The one big downside of this kind of business entity is that it doesn't offer any liability protection. If someone were to sue your business or if creditors come after you for some reason, all your business's assets as well as your personal assets would be at risk.

Partnership

A partnership has basically the same structure as a sole proprietorship. The difference is that a partnership has two or more owners. If you are putting together a partnership, you should draw up a legal document outlining the roles and responsibilities of each partner within the business. This document should include how profits and expenses will be divided and how the partnership can be dissolved.

LLC

Another option that many crafters take is to set up a limited liability corporation, or LLC. Setting up an LLC is more costly than forming a sole proprietorship or partnership, but it offers you more protection. The LLC is a separate entity from you and must be treated as such—meaning you'll have to open a business bank account and file business taxes. An LLC can have as many owner-members as you like, and it provides a protective legal barrier between your business assets and your personal assets.

Jon Wye creates graphic leather belts, wallets, and screen-printed T-shirts out of his studio in Washington, DC. At the very beginning of 2004, Jon decided he was going to start his company. "I was going to be official, and I was going to do it the right way," he explains. He read up on incorporation and found out what he needed to do to become a licensed and registered business. He thought it would be cute, and a good way to start a new year, to register on January 1. Unfortunately, the business office was closed for the holiday. "So I went back the next day, January second, and gave them all my papers and paid my little money and became an LLC. Then I had no idea what to do with myself after that."

What started out as a fun idea for Christmas presents quickly turned into a serious craft business for Kasey and Kelly Evick, of Biggs and Featherbelle. In December 2002, the sisters, who are based in Baltimore, Maryland, decided to make soap for holiday presents for their family. They soon realized they wanted to do something more with their soap creations, and so at the beginning of 2003, they got themselves organized and became an LLC. But then they slowed down. "We took the business very slow," explains Kasey. "The first year we developed recipes and did product development and research. We didn't even make products for the first six months." After creating their soaps, body butter bars, and lip balms, they began selling them at craft shows and then started to sell online. Their business began to feel real to them.

In 2004, they registered their business name, Biggs and Featherbelle, with the state of Maryland and filed for a federal tax ID (an employer identification number, or EIN) so they could sell wholesale. As their business has grown, they have not changed its legal structure. "We are still an LLC, and we still split everything fifty-fifty," Kasey says.

There are a couple of other organizational forms that your business could take, including the S corporation and the C corporation, but it is very rare to find an independently owned craft business organized as such. These business types are more costly to set up and run and are taxed at a much higher rate.

Ask a Lawyer

Before deciding how to organize your business, you may want to seek the advice of a lawyer. While this may seem scary to some, finding legal help can be easy and may help you avoid common mistakes that can cost you in the long run. As you start out in your crafting career, you may not have a lot of cash to spend on attorney's fees. Luckily there are several legal resources available specifically for those with low incomes or who are pursuing a creative career.

Volunteer Lawyers for the Arts

Volunteer Lawyers for the Arts specializes in pro bono legal help for low-income artists and arts organizations. The great thing about VLA is that the organization specializes in helping artists and crafters. VLA lawyers are familiar with the kinds of legal help crafters and artists typically need.

Chapters of the VLA are located throughout the United States, but unfortunately not everywhere. If you live in a state with a VLA chapter, you can probably access services via a VLA legal clinic, where you can speak with an attorney regarding more minor legal matters such as contract reviews or copyright claim questions. Local VLAs also may offer intake and referral services, placing you with a member attorney if you need longer-term legal help. To take advantage of the pro bono referral program, you have to meet certain income requirements, so check to make sure you qualify and follow all the intake and application requirements carefully.

Many VLA chapters also offer educational sessions, such as copyright and trademark workshops and sessions on nonprofit incorporation. These sessions are open to the public and to VLA members free of charge or for a very low admission fee.

State Bar Associations

Each state has a bar association—the statewide governing body that certifies lawyers to practice law. You may want to check with your local bar association to see whether it sponsors legal clinics, similar to those offered by the VLA, or provides pro bono intake referrals. Be aware, though, that the lawyers working at state bar associations' legal clinics may not be as familiar as VLA lawyers with the issues crafters typically face, and take that into account when researching your local bar's services.

University Law Schools

If you live near a university that has a law school, you may want to see whether the law school offers legal clinics to the community. These operate differently from the clinics provided by the VLA and by state bar associations. You apply for help, and law students in a particular course take on your case. (The benefit to students is that they get to learn how to assist various clients with their legal needs.) Acceptance into the clinic will be based on students' availability and on the time of the year. You'll need to research the intake process to find out at what points in the year (or semester) the clinic accepts new cases. The students will help your current legal need—sometimes extending their assistance into the next semester—but that's it. Since they are only students, you won't have an ongoing relationship with a law firm, which you might need.

A Crafty Education

The handmade community is a diverse and welcoming place—and people come to it from many different backgrounds. Sue Eggen, of Philadelphia, originally studied veterinary medicine, but now she makes and sells recycled-sweater hats and starlet crown headpieces under her business name, Giant Dwarf. San Francisco–based artist and illustrator Lisa Congdon started out in the nonprofit world. Tina Henry, who is based in Washington, DC, and makes zombie cards, magnets, and T-shirts under the name Tina Seamonster, studied journalism while in school.

There are crafters who have pursued fine arts (or fine arts and crafts) degrees, but many others have taken up their specific crafts on their own and are wholly self-taught. You don't need a master in fine arts (MFA) degree or any formal arts or crafts training to sell your handmade work, of course. That said, there may be educational opportunities that would be useful to you and that it may be worth your while

to explore. You just need to know where to look and how you learn best.

For learning specific skills, the Internet has opened up a 24/7 craft classroom. Blogs offer up crafters' personal experiences, and anyone can watch YouTube and Vimeo video tutorials. Craft schools such as Penland School of Crafts, in Penland, North Carolina; the Haystack Mountain School of Crafts, in Deer Isle, Maine; and the Arrowmont School of Arts and Crafts, in Gatlinburg, Tennessee, offer classes and workshops in a wide range of crafts—as do some local crafts supplies stores and arts organizations.

There are also numerous places to increase your business knowledge. Community colleges offer business classes. Etsy's I Heart Art programs partner with colleges and museums to offer artists and crafters resources for improving their business skills. And, as an outcome of a grant-funded study of business models like Etsy's, the Maryland Institute College of Art (MICA) now offers a graduate master in professional studies (MPS) degree in the business of art and design. Through its study, MICA found that while most independent businesses fail as fast as they begin, about 87 percent of the owners of the ones that do succeed have some sort of business training. Chris Herring, of MICA's graduate admissions office, explains that the program—the first of its kind in the country—has two parts: the first is about learning the business fundamentals, while the second is about taking all you've learned in the first and applying it to your own specific creative work.

Crafty business conferences are also popping up all over the place. The first was the Craft Congress held in 2007 in Philadelphia. And today you can choose from a number of crafts-oriented business conferences, including the Summit of Awesome, among others. There are also Etsy's virtual labs and a plethora of online courses and business books such as Kari Chapin's *The Handmade Marketplace*—and, of course, this one!

Through its study, MICA found that while most independent businesses fail as fast as they begin, about 87 percent of the owners of the ones that do succeed have some sort of business training.

In short, there are learning opportunities around every corner. You have to decide which options are worth your investment of time and money at this point in your crafty career. The skills and education you need when you are first starting out are different from what you'll need when you are further along in your business. As writer Richard Bach has said: "Learning is finding out what you already know. Doing is demonstrating that you know it. Teaching is reminding others that they know it as well as you do. We are all learners, doers, and teachers." To sustain the creative community and keep it growing, we must all keep learning, doing, and teaching.

Owning Your Awesome

Reality can be harsh, and customers can be cruel. How many of you have heard a customer say of your work, "Oh, I could make that"? But you need to believe in yourself and what you are doing to be really successful. You need drive, passion, and determination to make it as an entrepreneur.

Scary, right? Yes, but think about how good it feels to be striking out on your own, pursuing the life you want to live, and creating amazing things. Remember that there will be many supporters as well as detractors along the way, and don't let the negative nellies get to you.

It takes time to learn and hone your craft and to turn it into a truly amazing kick-ass business, but once you get there you need to *own your awesome*. Too many amazing and accomplished crafters don't believe that their unique experience qualifies them as experts.

What's the first thing you do when someone points to your awesome coffee mug and asks if you made it? Or when someone compliments you on your silk-screened T-shirts? Do you say yes, and then qualify the statement with a shrug and an "it's no big deal" attitude?

If you're guilty of this practice, stop it. Stop it right now.

By demurring, refusing the compliment, and shaking off the praise, you're teaching that potential customer to treat your very hard work—and the work of the handmade community in general—without the respect and reverence it deserves. You're telling them that it's no big deal. But in reality it is a big deal—a *BFD*, even.

So own it. Get your "elevator pitch" down. Say thank you when complimented, and open the door to a sale to a potential evangelist who may spread your handmade goodness to others, leading to even more sales.

Be realistic, but don't be hard on yourself. You are amazing, doing super-awesome, super-amazing things. Be proud of your accomplishments, because you've worked your ass off to get there. Sometimes you're going to be the only one who believes in what you're doing. But stand strong. As crafter Jon Wye says, "It's easy if you don't try, but if you want to get the girl, you have to put yourself out there."

Chapter

3

LEARNING THE
NUTS & BOLTS

C reating and making are fun, but there's another side to running a craft business—the administrative side. Hopefully, by now you know which kind of legal structure is best for your business and whether you need a business license. But there are various other nuts and bolts that are crucial: arranging for credit card payments, keeping inventory, doing accounting, paying taxes, registering for copyright and trademark, and getting health insurance and other benefits. These tasks can be taxing (pun intended) and are often neglected, but they are necessary for a healthy craft business.

Getting Paid

If your crafts are appealing, people are going to want to give you money for them. Your job is to make it easy for them to do so. Offering a number of different payment options may be critical to your business's success.

Cash

The most basic method of payment is cold hard cash. Although accepting cash is the easiest way to get paid, it can also be the most difficult to track. You'll most likely accept cash via direct person-to-person sales. Be sure to keep track of every cash transaction, and at the end of the day (or as soon as possible), deposit the total amount.

Checks

You'll undoubtedly receive checks as payment for invoices or large orders, but it is up to you to decide whether you also want to accept checks when you sell at craft fairs. When accepting a check for any person-to-person sale, be sure to review the information on the check with the buyer. Ask if the name and address on the check are correct and current; if the buyer's phone number isn't on the check, ask the buyer for it, and write it on the check. As an extra precaution, ask for ID. Review the information to make sure it

matches the information on the check. Be sure to deposit all checks at the end of the day or as soon as possible. The biggest downside to accepting checks is the possibility that they may bounce. This is where that phone number comes in handy. If a check does bounce, you'll have to call and ask the buyer to reissue the check—including any bank fees you may have incurred.

PayPal

The online payment system PayPal is ubiquitous within the DIY marketplace, and if you're going to be a part of the handmade economy, you'll need to set up a PayPal

Business Planning

Sitting down and actually planning out your craft business may seem like a big time-suck, but spending just a little time on this up front can save you a lot of time down the road. And while an actual "business plan" may seem intimidating, just setting down a simple outline can help clarify a path to success.

At a minimum, a plan should include the following items:

- **An explanation of what your craft business is about.** What are you going to make or sell and where?
- **Market research.** Who else is making these things, and how will your brand and products be different? Who do you want to sell to? Who is your ideal audience?
- **Business type.** How are you going to organize your business? What form should it take? Will you be the only owner? Will you have a partner? Will you have need for employees one day?
- **Marketing.** How do you plan to market your craft? Will you need a Facebook page? A website?
- **An outline of your product line.** What do you plan to make? Where will you source your materials? How much time will you have to spend on production versus selling?
- **Finances.** How much money will you need to start your business? Can you afford an all-out marketing push, or will you have to invest slowly and over time? How much do you have to sell to make a profit in a month? Three months? Six months? One year?

No matter how much time you put into your business planning, keep in mind that your plan can and should be flexible, as some things won't go as planned—the market may take a downturn, or you may need to invest more time in the business because of an unexpected uptick in sales. Learn to roll with the punches, and be ready to take the opportunities as they come.

account. (It's easy to do: Go to Paypal.com, click on "Getting Started," and follow the steps.) PayPal allows you to receive and send money easily, as well as to accept credit card payments. Etsy, the go-to online store for crafters, uses PayPal for checkout. You can also put PayPal payment buttons on your own website, and PayPal even has an app that allows customers to send you money instantly via their smartphones. PayPal charges some small fees for transactions, but these are a minor annoyance—just part of the cost of doing business online.

Credit and Debit Cards

Fortunately, accepting credit cards (and debit cards that act just like credit cards) has become more user-friendly than it used to be. Deciding where you plan to accept them will determine which service is right for you. If you plan to sell only online, PayPal provides the easiest way to accept credit and debit cards. Because PayPal is so prevalent in the handmade community, customers are accustomed to using it. PayPal's interface is easy to understand, and the service is very reliable.

But you may also want to give customers the option of paying by credit/debit card when you sell at craft fairs. Remember, you want to make it *easy* for shoppers to give you money, and many will opt to pay with their credit or debit cards rather than cash if given the opportunity.

There are several options you can choose from. The first is to set up a merchant account with your bank or a credit card terminal service. One popular such service is ProPay. When you set up a ProPay account, you can choose among several levels of service. You will more than likely have to pay a setup fee, as well as a fee for the card reader that transmits the payment information, transaction fees, and a monthly or yearly fee for the use of the account. Be sure to review all the costs involved before deciding. Though the fees may seem like a lot, if you compare those costs with the sales you may lose because you don't accept credit cards, you may decide that having the ability to take cards wins out. With a service like ProPay, you have the option to accept credit/debit card payments and to process those payments online, over the phone, or through your smartphone.

Another option is Square, which is quickly becoming the go-to service for crafters who have smartphones or a tablet. Square, which burst onto the scene in 2010, charges no sign-up fees, device fees, or annual fees, and its transaction fees are low. Even the app is free, making credit card payments accessible to many who cannot afford a merchant account. Needless to say, crafters have been adopting Square at an exponential rate.

Square's card reader attaches to your smartphone or tablet and is compatible with Apple's iPhones and iPads as well as with Google's Android devices. You will need cell reception or Wi-Fi to process your transactions, just as you would with a merchant account device. Square makes it easy to add sales tax to your transactions if you are required to collect it, and you can also use the app to record cash payments on your smartphone or tablet. These features help keep you organized, and it is a great timesaver to have a record of all of your transactions at the end of a long day. You can also export a CSV (comma-separated values) file of all of your transactions to a spreadsheet to help with your bookkeeping.

The other great thing about Square is that it creates e-mail or text-message receipts, providing your customers with information on the purchased item and the seller, along with a map of where the transaction took place.

Unfortunately, sometimes you won't have access to Wi-Fi, or, worse, your mobile device will malfunction, which means you need a backup. That backup comes in the form of what is lovingly known as a "knuckle buster"— the manual card-imprinting

machine that carries your business information on an embossed metal plate and allows you to create paper receipts for yourself and your customers. At the end of the day, you will need to manually enter all the credit card information you acquired, so use this method only as a backup.

Another thing to keep in mind when choosing a method for accepting credit cards is how the service handles the various credit and debit cards out there. There may be different fees for running a MasterCard versus a Discover card. Or your service might not accept American Express cards at all. Review the terms of service carefully before deciding which service is best for you.

Pricing Your Work

When pricing your work, don't set prices based solely on what you think will sell. People who've bought into the bargain-seeking attitude of our culture are always on the lookout for cut-rate prices and "deals," but catering to the lowest common denominator is not sustainable for handmade businesses. Not everyone can afford handmade items, but that's not your fault. If this reality makes you unhappy, consider adding items that have low production costs so you have some more affordable options in your line. But, bottom line, you have to honor the value of your work, factor in your expenses and profit goals, and understand your customer base when setting prices. You may have to educate shoppers about the creative inspiration, meticulous process, and love that go into each item you make. By highlighting the benefits of buying handmade, you'll help customers understand how their dollars foster you as an artist and your local community.

Okay. Get out the calculator. Here comes the math part.

In "The Art of Pricing" section of Etsy's online *Seller Handbook,* Danielle Maveal shows how to use your output level to set the average per-item price you'll need to achieve your yearly revenue goal. Here's the exercise she gives for determining this "suggestive" price

1. Decide what you want your yearly gross sales to be.

2. Figure out how many items you make per week, and how many for an entire year.

3. Divide your gross sales goal by the number of items you can create. (For example, perhaps you'd like to sell $12,000 worth of goods. If you make 5 items a week, you will make approximately 250 items. Dividing $12,000 by 250 items would give you a $50 price point.)

Although Maveal's suggestive-price formula will help you determine whether you are pricing your work appropriately, she also points out that "a pricing formula should really be unique to you and your work. There really isn't a formula that works for everyone. It's a little bit of taking a piece you want from this formula and taking a little bit of that."

Once you have a suggestive price, focus on profitability. (Keep in mind that Maveal's formula uses *gross* sales revenue, so you'll need to cover expenses before you see any profit.) First, add up all your expenses, including labor, materials, and overhead, to determine a base whole-sale price, then double that number for a profitable retail price.

Megan Auman, a jewelry designer and metalsmith, has written extensively about pricing and value. In *Skill, Price, and Profit: The Best of Crafting an MBA* (which you can find on craftmba.com), Auman provides these formulas:

$$labor + materials + overhead + profit = wholesale\ price$$

$$wholesale\ price \times 2\ (at\ a\ minimum) = retail\ price$$

To figure out your labor cost, Maveal suggests reviewing an online salary calculator on a site like Freelanceswitch.com, Indeed.com, or Salary.com to see what a designer or seamstress in your area makes per hour. But she cautions, "There are a lot of other factors to consider." You should figure in the time it took you to develop your product line, the time and cost of any relevant education, and any special factors— for example, if a technique you use was passed down through your family. As Maveal explains, "I always say your price should also tell a story. If you have a price where people are going to say, 'Oh, why is that $300?', you can tell them in your item description all the different elements that went into that piece."

If you're just starting out, Maveal suggests setting your prices on the high end: "It is easier to drop your prices if something's not working than to raise them. If you're always raising your prices, people are going to notice, but it's easier to drop them down a little bit."

Maveal also says it is important to think about where you want your business to go, and if wholesaling is part of your long-term plan, you'll need to set your prices accordingly so you're prepared for that growth. As Auman observes, "When most makers start pricing their products, they aren't hitting all four areas that add up to wholesale price. . . . More often than not, by the time you add up labor + materials + overhead, you forget to add that all-important last element, profit." Stressing the importance of profit, Auman underlines the difference between profit and hourly rate, and the need to account for both: "Your hourly rate is what funnels into your personal account to help you pay for things like food and your mortgage. But profit is money that gets invested directly back into the business." (And, by the way, if you're tempted to use an item's wholesale price when selling online or at craft fairs, don't do it! You will be undervaluing yourself and most likely undercutting your fellow crafters, as well.)

Pricing is an evolution, so once you set your prices, the job is not done. Auman encourages business owners to "look at your pricing structure, continually reevaluate your finances, and figure out if the prices you're charging and the money you're bringing in are truly enough to support the ways you'd like your company to grow."

Honestly assessing your company's finances may seem tedious and scary—or overwhelming—but it is an essential step in establishing price points that will sustain the long-term growth of your business. If you absolutely cannot do the math, consider hiring an accountant or a small-business consultant to help you.

How Much Do You Need to Sell?

To get a rough idea of the number of items you'll need to sell over the course of the year to meet your revenue goal, try this formula, derived from *Skill, Price, and Profit*, by Megan Auman.

desired profit + desired annual salary + projected annual material and overhead expenses = revenue goal

revenue goal ÷ current price =
number of products you need to sell

Keeping Inventory

Once you start selling, you're going to have to keep track of your inventory. Setting up a process right now for tracking products and sales will save you headaches in the future. A simple Excel spreadsheet with headers for product name, quantity, wholesale price, retail price, and place of sale is a good start. Include each item you make on the spreadsheet, taking care to keep separate inventories for online sales (including sales at different online shops) and offline sales to avoid double-selling an item—especially important if an item is one of a kind. Update the spreadsheet regularly—after each online sale and after each day of sales at a craft fair. You can, of course, trade offline inventory for online inventory, or vice versa. If you've made too many items for a craft fair and want to sell the leftover items online, do so. Just make sure you track each such change in your inventory spreadsheet. And make sure to delist any online items before you offer them for sale offline.

You may also want to set up a simple spreadsheet for your materials and supplies. This can help you see when you are getting low and need to reorder before you run out.

Accounting

No one likes accounting, but it is a necessary evil. Get in the habit now of keeping track of your incoming and outgoing money to avoid pulling your hair out during tax season. Save all the receipts associated with your business, and set a regular time every two weeks, month, or quarter to go over your books and organize them. Keeping to this schedule will give you a better overview of where your money is going and how healthy your business is financially.

Several programs are available to help you keep track of your expenses and income. You can set up with a simple Excel spreadsheet, or you can use a more advanced system such as QuickBooks, which can connect with your bank accounts, produce invoices, keep track of expenses, and apply sales taxes. Another option is Outright, an online program that connects to your bank accounts and helps you estimate quarterly taxes. And yet another option for organizing your business's finances is Mint. This free online service features easy-to-understand charts and graphs to help you see where your money is going.

All these programs make it easy for you to do your own bookkeeping. You just have to be disciplined enough to keep an eye on it all. If, for whatever reason, you can't, it may make sense for you to hire a bookkeeper.

Lee Meredith, who sells knit kits and a variety of crafts at leethal.net, uses a very detailed Excel spreadsheet to keep track of her income and expenses and updates it quarterly. Artist and illustrator Lisa Congdon does her own bookkeeping every two weeks but has an accountant prepare and file her quarterly taxes. "Being self-employed and having to pay quarterly taxes has been a wake-up call for me. People don't really talk about how hard it

is to save money for taxes," says Lisa. And Shauna Alterio, who sells hand-carved Mustaches on a Stick and other novelty crafts under the name Something's Hiding in Here, explains that by keeping track of your receipts and paying attention to where you spend your money, you are able to "look at those decisions and start to figure out where you can save money and where you really want to spend that money." We can't stress enough how important it is to keep accurate books and to regularly take an honest look at your finances. It will help you in the long run.

Paying Taxes

As you transition to owning your own business, you'll have to deal with taxes differently from the way you used to. For tax purposes, you'll have to keep track of all of your business's expenses and income. You'll probably have to pay quarterly estimated taxes. You'll be responsible for paying all your FICA (Federal Insurance Contributions Act) taxes—the federal taxes that go toward Social Security and Medicare. You may have to pay sales tax. And your yearly tax returns are likely to become much more complicated than they were when you worked for somebody else.

Quarterly Taxes

You are now responsible for paying all the taxes that an employer ordinarily removes from an employee's paycheck: federal and state income taxes as well as FICA taxes. When your business is organized as a sole proprietorship, FICA taxes are referred to as the *self-employment tax*, covering contributions to both Medicare and Social Security. Newly self-employed people sometimes find this part of the tax law especially burdensome: If you were working for somebody else, your employer would be responsible for paying half of your FICA tax bill; as a self-employed person, however, you must pay the *whole* self-employment tax, which in 2011 stood at 13.3 percent of your earnings up to $106,800.

You are expected to pay these taxes as an estimated tax on a quarterly basis. Then, at tax time, you'll file as self-employed, reporting all tax payments and deducting all business expenses from the previous year. It is extremely important to pay your estimated quarterly taxes; if you do not, you

may find that, come April 15, you cannot afford to pay the lump sum for the total tax you owe, and the IRS may assess penalties if you have not paid enough in quarterly taxes. To be able to pay your quarterly estimated taxes on time, you'll have to get in the habit of saving a percentage of the money you get from each sale you make. The percentage is based on your total estimated income, and in the beginning it may be hard for you to judge just how much you should save and pay each quarter. Some self-employed crafters also find it psychologically difficult to have income coming in but not being able to spend it. As Lisa Congdon explains, "Income is flexible—one month you do really well, and the next month you hardly have enough to live on, so you have to think a lot about saving. You learn to live within your means."

If you have organized your business as an LLC, you will be paying yourself as an employee throughout the year, deducting taxes from your paychecks,

and then filing a regular W-2 form come tax time. Although you won't be filing as self-employed, you in essence will still be responsible for paying all your taxes yourself. A payroll service such as ADP can help with your tax accounting if you are an employee of your business or have other employees beside yourself.

To avoid fees and penalties, it is very important that you consult with a tax professional to make sure you are filing correctly. At the very minimum, check out the IRS website (irs.gov), which is chock full of very helpful tax information that can give you a basic understanding, so you're not completely lost in this area.

Federal Tax ID

You may also be required to obtain a federal tax ID, or employer identification number (EIN), for your business, especially if it is organized as an LLC or you plan to buy or sell wholesale, open a business bank account, or hire employees. You can easily apply for an EIN online via the IRS website, irs.gov. Even if your business is a sole proprietorship, it may behoove you to apply for an EIN so you can protect your Social Security number when doing business.

Sales Tax

Your state may require you to collect and pay sales tax on your in-person retail sales. If so, you'll have to acquire a sales tax ID and add a percentage to each transaction, saving that percentage and reporting and paying the total amount to your state on either a monthly or a quarterly basis. The sales tax rate differs from state to state, so be sure that when you apply for your sales tax ID, you make note of your state's sales tax law and deadlines. To find out how to obtain your sales tax ID, check with your state's department of taxation or revenue.

If you sell online, you currently have to collect and pay sales tax only if you have a physical location (a retail shop, warehouse, office, or studio) in your state and are selling online to someone who lives in your state. When you sell online to customers who are out of state, the burden of paying their state's sales tax technically falls on them.

When you sell at a craft fair, the fair's organizers should let you know whether you are responsible for collecting sales tax during that fair. If you are required to do so, the organizers should also provide you with all the information you need to collect sales tax and pay it to the proper state authority.

Getting Tax Help

If you've made it this far without your eyes rolling back in your head, congratulations! You may find deciphering your business's finances and understanding your tax obligations is fun—but if you would rather stick knitting needles in your eyes than keep a spreadsheet and prepare your taxes, then getting a bookkeeper and/or accountant may be the best investment you can make.

Income is flexible—one month you do really well, and the next month you hardly have enough to live on, so you have to think a lot about saving. You learn to live within your means.

—LISA CONGDON, artist and illustrator

Copyright and Trademark

There are several mechanisms in US law for protecting your ownership of the original work you create. *Copyright* protects the designs and objects that you, as a crafter, make. *Trademark* protects the "marks" of your brand—including your business's name, your logo, and the names of your products or product lines. You don't have to register for either copyright or trademark, but it might be worth your while to do so.

Registering Copyright

As the creator of your own work, you own it and have the rights to reproduce and make copies of the work; to distribute and sell it and give others permission to do so; to create or license derivative or modified works (such as plush toys based on illustrations); and to display your work publicly.

To claim copyright for your work, your creation must be original and must be fixed in a "tangible medium of expression," as the law puts it. Once your original work has been created (knit, sewn, drawn, printed, thrown, or whatever), it automatically acquires copyright protection. While this is useful, it offers little legal protection. To gain greater legal protection of your work, you should register your work's copyright with the US Copyright Office.

Basic copyright registration costs $35, and if your work is "unpublished"—which for crafters means that you have not sold it or exhibited it in public—you can complete registration online. If, however, your work has been "published," you must deliver a copy or "best edition" of your work to be held on record at the Library of Congress. For more information on copyright, consult the Copyright Office's website, copyright.gov.

Why Register Your Copyright?

Since your work automatically obtains copyright protection once it's been created, you may be wondering why you should take the extra step of registering your work. Well, registration offers the "author" (which is what you, the creator, are known as in copyright law) several advantages:

- It establishes a public record of your work.
- It establishes the legal presumption that the work is yours.
- It enables you to bring suit against an alleged infringer in federal court.
- It enables you to sue for presumptive damages instead of just actual damages (which is the case if your work is not registered).
- It gives you the option of petitioning the court to require the infringer to pay your legal and court fees.
- It gives you the option of asking for an injunction against further infringement, which could include seizure and destruction of any infringing products.

While you are no longer required to include a copyright notice (the © copyright symbol as well as the year of copyright and the copyright holder's name) on your work, it is beneficial to do so, because it warns others against copying your work without your permission.

Copyright Infringement

If you suspect someone of copying your original designs, sending them an e-mail message or letter asking them to stop may do the trick. Word such correspondence very carefully, however. You don't want to get yourself in a situation in which you can't enforce baseless claims. In order to prove copyright infringement in a court of law, you'll have to demonstrate three things:

1. You must prove that you are the "author" (i.e., the creator) of the original work.
2. If the work is not clearly identical, you must prove the alleged infringer has or had access to the original and has copied it.
3. Again, if the work is not identical, you must show sufficient similarities between your work and that of the alleged infringer. This means showing "actual similarities" or similarities that an "ordinary person" could see.

Do note that no one can claim copyright of a fact, such as the appearance of an owl or a cupcake. What you *can* claim copyright of is your original interpretation or expression of an owl or a cupcake. It's also important to note that copyright law is highly complicated. Infringement isn't necessarily a black-and-white matter. A copy may be considered "fair use" if the work is used for purposes of criticism, commentary, reporting, teaching, research, or parody.

If you believe that someone is knocking off your work and that you are really being damaged by the copying, seek the advice of an attorney. But be aware that with the widespread availability of designs through the Internet, copying has become epidemic, and you probably won't be able to keep on top of those who steal your designs. If you worry too much about possible copiers and close yourself off from good exposure, you'll only be hurting your business.

Copycats

Simply by putting your creations out into the world, you're likely to have copycats. The best way to deal with copiers is to keep your brand and product line evolving. If you do encounter copiers, it's important to keep true to yourself, to your brand, and to the reason you got into the business in the first place. You don't want to put yourself in a position where you are in competition with your copiers.

Shauna Alterio and Stephen Loidolt of Something's Hiding in Here have had to deal with copycats. When they started making their signature Mustache on a Stick, no one else was making anything like it, and their business from that one product was great. But, Shauna, says, "There are so many people who are making similar goods now. Theirs are slightly different in aesthetic and slightly less expensive. So we've definitely seen where we've had to focus. We still love this thing and still feel really confident

that the way we're doing it is the best way. We think that our materials are the most sophisticated, our craft is the best that it can be, and we're not going to compromise. We are not going to just charge less for it because other people are. We are going to trust that if people are interested in Stephen and me and in Something's Hiding, they are going to invest in the best version. And the other people who want something cheaper are going to buy the cheaper thing."

Shauna also says that she and Stephen are always "looking for the next thing." In 2010, they had the opportunity to do a show at the Curiosity Shop in San Francisco. They ended up creating bow ties for that show, and their Forage Bow Tie line was born. A year later, business from their bow tie line accounted for about 50 percent of their business. Theirs is a good example of a business open to evolving and growing. Shauna explains, "If we ran a business solely focused on one item, we would definitely be in trouble, and we would end up competing with the people who started to duplicate what we were doing. We don't ever want to end up in that position because we don't want to end up compromising."

If you yourself are accused of copying, it's important to keep a level head and assess the situation. How were you notified? Via e-mail from another crafter or a letter from an attorney? If an attorney, you should consult one of your own straight away. If crafter to crafter, you can be a bit more informal, but be careful about what you say in your correspondence and never be afraid to bring in an attorney if things escalate. Be sure that you're dating your sketchbooks and keeping records on when you debut your product lines. These measures will help in sussing out timelines, but know that it is entirely possible that two people can come up with a very similar idea or design at the same time.

Why Register a Trademark?

Registering your logo, business name, and/or product names with the US Patent and Trademark Office provides you with a number of legal advantages:

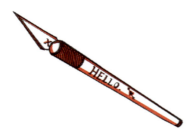

- It establishes a public record of your "mark."
- It establishes legal presumption that you own the trademarked element.
- It gives you the ability to bring suit against an alleged infringer in federal court.
- It gives you the right to use the ® (registered trademark) symbol.
- Your mark gets listed in the federal trademark database.
- You can use your US registration to obtain registration in a foreign country.

Registering a Trademark

Trademark offers a different sort of protection from copyright. Whereas copyright protects individual works, trademark covers "a word, phrase, symbol, or design"— a business's name, or slogan, or logo. Trademarks are regulated by the US Patent and Trademark Office, and, similarly to copyright, your "mark" acquires protection upon creation. But also as with copyright, this unregistered "mark" grants less legal protection than a registered mark.

Trademark application costs between $275 and $325, depending on the class or type of "mark" you apply for. While it is not a requirement when applying for trademark registration, we strongly recommend you perform a search of the Patent and Trademark database for prior use of the trademark you wish to register. Showing that there are no registered marks (or pending registrations of marks) that are similar to yours will strengthen your application. Also, the Patent and Trademark

Office will search for similar marks *after* you apply for your mark, and the office will deny your registration if similar marks are found. So it helps to conduct this research before you submit your application so you don't waste your money and so you can take steps to strengthen your application or decide to go in another direction altogether.

While you do not need to hire an attorney to search the database and file the application for each mark, we recommend that you do, as the registration process is complicated. It can also become quite expensive. A cursory search might cost $75, but a more in-depth search can cost up to $500 per mark. You may have sticker shock for the amount of money you'll spend on registering your mark, but it is worth it if your business is taking off and you find yourself in the limelight. The more exposure you have, the more important it is to be legally protected.

Arranging for Health Insurance and Other Benefits

For self-employed people, including crafters, benefits can too often seem like a luxury item. Because individual health, dental, and disability insurance policies are so expensive, many crafters go without. You sit around hoping you don't get sick or hurt in an accident. Regular dental cleanings become a thing of the past, and flossing becomes an almost compulsive disorder in your effort to not get cavities. And, God forbid, if you do get sick or hurt and can't work for an extended period of time, you might be looking at bounced rent checks and a cold, hungry winter.

Many crafters also let retirement plans fall by the wayside. Yes, there are individual IRA options, but they can be confusing. And, hey, retirement is in the distant future anyway, and something will have changed by then, right?

If you're lucky, your spouse or partner has a conventional job, is building a retirement nest egg, and can get you covered on his or her health and dental plan. But if that's not the case, don't despair. There are a couple of options that you, as an individual, can pursue.

In membership organizations like the Freelancers Union, the Graphic Artists Guild, the American Craft Council, and the Craft and Hobby Association, many self-employed individuals have joined together, like a company, to arrange for benefits such as group health insurance, disability and life insurance, and 401(k) retirement plans. Are these plans as good as what you could get working for someone else? Probably not. Could you possibly get something better on your own? Maybe. But the plans these organizations offer are adequate, and you'll probably find something suitable to your budget. To find out more about the organizations, eligibility and membership requirements, and the specifics of the benefit plans they offer, consult their websites.

And don't completely discount the feasibility of individual plans. While you may suffer sticker shock when you look at the premiums, it is scarier to come down with a serious illness and have to forgo treatment because you can't afford it. The Affordable Care Act, which became law in 2010, will help bring health care costs down and will be beneficial to self-employed crafters and employee-based small businesses. The law won't take full effect, however, until 2014; consult Healthcare.gov for more information.

Portland, Oregon–based illustrator Ryan Berkley quit his day job in 2011 to focus full time on his and his wife's crafty business. The fear of not having health insurance was what had held them back, but they were finally able to work it out. As Ryan's wife, Lucy, explains, "We just budgeted it and realized that it was a business expense and hoped the amount of money that we would be able to make by having that extra time would work out to pay the insurance bill."

Of course, if you have a larger business with several employees, you may qualify for group health or dental plans. But that doesn't mean your troubles are over, since paying health plan premiums can be problematic even for well-established indie crafters. Another Portland-based craft business, Queen Bee Creations, has found health insurance to be a tough hill to climb. When the economic downturn happened, owner Rebecca Pearcy had to reassess: "We had to lay off two people, and we had to cut our health insurance and our dental insurance, which we had worked really hard to get and to provide to our employees." And even when the market started to come around and Queen Bee was able to rehire one person back, the company still couldn't reinstate its health insurance benefit. As Pearcy says, "We want to bring it back, but we haven't gotten to the point where it's possible financially."

Chapter

4

CREATING
SOMETHING
AWESOME

- -

The first and most important rule for creating a successful handmade business is that you need to *create something awesome*. There are thousands of other handmade sellers offering "unique" items, and the competition is too stiff for you to do anything less.

While it can take some time to find the right combination of awesomeness for your product line to be noticed and then take off, taking the time to figure out the best combination will be worth the effort. While "awesomeness" is subjective, there are a few criteria for judging whether your idea for a product line fits the bill.

Having a Passion for Your Work

Passion is the first ingredient in awesomeness. You need to have a passion for your work, not just because you're making it but because it has some greater significance to you and the life you value.

When your product line is an extension of your values, you may find a community of like-minded people who may become your customers. For example, say you love craft beer and devise a way to incorporate the cool-looking bottle caps from beers you enjoy into a line of products geared toward beer enthusiasts. Instead of "selling," you'll be talking to people about stuff that truly excites you. And the people who express interest will probably have some connection to craft beer and will be interested in the same things you are—the imagery on the bottle caps, the styles of beer represented, the locations of the breweries, and so on.

Lots of people in the crafts world have this kind of personal passion: bike enthusiasts who start their own line of bike gear and cycling fashion accessories, avid knitters who publish their own patterns, and eco-warriors who make clever products for more sustainable living. One such crafter is Becky Striepe, of Atlanta-based Glue and Glitter, who makes a line of eco-friendly home goods for the kitchen. As she explained on the *Hello Craft* blog, "The idea is to create products that help people reduce waste in their day-to-day without sacrificing style. Whether an apron encourages someone to get in the kitchen instead of ordering wasteful takeout, or a lunch bag gets you bringing your lunch to work or school without all of the disposables, I want to make sustainability fun and cute for kids and for grown-ups." Becky has always been passionate about the environment and runs her business with sustainability in mind: "All my fabrics are reclaimed, recycled, vintage, or organic. I save my scraps to use in other projects, and I aim to make products that help pass that value on to my customers."

Meeting a Need

When your products address a specific problem—whether people realize that it exists or not—they can meet a need both in your own life and in the lives of your customers. For example, say you want to reduce waste associated with plastic bags, so you start a line of handmade totes, fabric produce bags, or lunch kits. Or say you want to grow your own vegetables but have limited space, so you create container-garden kits designed for small-space living.

Or perhaps your favorite activity provides therapeutic benefits, but you recognize that the barriers that initially held you back may also prevent others from trying the activity, so you create a product that makes the activity more accessible. That was Jenny Hart's inspiration for her Sublime Stitching embroidery patterns and kits.

When Jenny first became intrigued by embroidery, she was put off by the seeming difficulty of embroidery techniques and by the lack of appealing pattern choices. (She didn't want to embroider bunnies or teddy bears.) But finally she decided to give it a try, using a sketch she'd made from a photo of her mother as her pattern.

Her mother taught her some basic stitches, and Jenny's whole world changed. She describes a "transformative experience of feeling total relaxation and concentration and the satisfaction of understanding how something that had intrigued me for so long worked, and going, 'This is so simple! This is so relaxing!'"

As she continued sketching her own designs to embroider, Jenny began to wonder whether there were other people who might discover the same rewarding experience if they had access to up-to-date designs and clear instructions. So Jenny set out to "get people interested in embroidery" by "starting a design company offering patterns that you couldn't get else-where" along with simple "instructions that explained embroidery in a way that I hadn't seen it explained before." Fast-forward several years, and Sublime Stitching has become a well-known brand in the indie craft community. Not only has Sublime Stitching removed a barrier for many would-be stitchers who were mystified by embroidery and itching for fun patterns, but it also offers seasoned stitchers a new and exciting approach to their work.

Telling a Story

Some of the best product lines and brands come from talented storytellers who make their products more meaningful through the stories they tell. Ryan and Lucy Berkley, the husband-and-wife team behind Berkley Illustration, found instant success with their line of prints featuring "animals, creatures, and friends." They opened their shop on Etsy in 2007, rang up more than a thousand sales in their first two months, and have now reached well over 25,000 sales while continuing to add to their extensive line. Ryan credits the descriptions they include in their product listings as one of the factors contributing to their success. The couple tells stories about their well-dressed animals to bring them to life, creating a playful world their customers enjoy. A few examples from the Berkleys' Etsy shop:

LADY RABBIT: This pretty lady travels with her husband, a magician, and often stars as his opening act. She has a wonderful one-woman band act playing the banjo, harmonica, and snare drum simultaneously. She also fills in the rim shots during his routine.

POLAR BEAR: Meet Willard the Polar Bear! This rosy fellow is the Chairman of the Board for a successful popsicle corporation. His ingenuity in the frozen novelty field is unsurpassed and he's currently working on a flavor that is so secret, he has to carry the recipe in a briefcase handcuffed to his arm.

CHEETAH: After cataract surgery ten years ago, this cheetah realized that an eye patch can be a real conversation starter with the ladies. His eye has long since healed but his social calendar remains quite full.

Tina Seamonster, based in Washington, DC, is another natural storyteller who finds inspiration for her product designs in the stories she has written about her life. Several of Tina's early designs feature quotes pulled from her numerous blog posts and tweets, including "Sometimes I Worry about Zombies," which has evolved into an entire line of gear, including T-shirts, magnets, and bookmarks.

Doing Market Research

When starting out, doing some basic research on the market you plan on entering is a necessity. The Internet is your friend here. Search standalone websites and Etsy shops for items similar to what you want to make and sell.

Say you want to make and sell jewelry. A quick search for the keyword *jewelry* on Google brings up about 867 million results, and a similar keyword search on Etsy yields well over 2 million items. Jewelry is obviously an overcrowded market! That doesn't mean you shouldn't pursue a jewelry line; it just means you'll have to work that much harder to make your jewelry special and to find a fan base to support you.

Another quick way to get a sense of the types of designs and products on the handmade market is to attend a few craft fairs. If you see products similar to what you want to make, consider going in a different direction, or work hard at making your product truly unique.

This research goes double for business and product names. Simple Google and Etsy searches should help you avoid using a name that is already taken or one that's too close to someone else's brand. You want your business name to be memorable—but not because it reminds people of somebody else's shop.

Developing a Product Line

Brands that have a cohesive product line stand out and have a better chance of enticing new customers with a complete look and of encouraging repeat customers to develop collections.

The more control you have over the design of all aspects of your product, the easier it will be to create a cohesive product line. Sometimes it's not possible to have total control over your materials, however, so be ready to get comfortable with compromise. One of the biggest challenges for a small business is to strike a profitable balance between creativity and compromise. Embrace the challenge, and always look for ways to use an advantage you may otherwise overlook.

Alison Dryer, of Baltimore-based Pistol Stitch Designs, created a line of handbags that were an instant hit, so she wanted to quickly add new designs to her collection. Finding the right fabrics was a breeze, but when it came to sourcing handles that would work for new styles she designed while also maintaining cohesion within her collection, she met a much greater challenge. Ali shared her frustration with a friend, who offered to help her get the handles she wanted made using the materials she preferred. Together, Ali and her friend

were able to produce a line of handles that fit in seamlessly with her entire handbag collection. Creative collaboration was all she needed to overcome an obstacle, and Ali's story serves as a reminder that being resourceful sometimes simply means sharing your problems with friends and bouncing around ideas in search of a workable solution.

Diane Koss, of Philadelphia-based Cutesy But Not Cutesy, started with a line of hand-sewn plush monsters and quickly began looking for ways to expand her product line. She saw that sales would rise if she expanded her original line to include practical items like shirts and dinnerware featuring her monster designs. As she explains, "With my plush toys, there are a lot of adults that like them, but they couldn't seem to find a reason to buy themselves a monster. So I started thinking of different ways they could have the characters. That's when I came up with the dishes and mugs, things an adult could use. Adults like the characters because it brings out the kid in them, but they want more useful items."

Although they didn't set out with the intention of creating a line that would encourage collecting, Lucy and Ryan Berkley observed that some customers were purchasing several of their Berkley illustration prints at a time—as if they were buying a series. The pair realized that they could play to that strength as they released new designs. One thing they did was to let customers vote on which animals they wanted to see next, which helped the Berkleys ensure that the new products they released already had a built-in fan base. By paying attention to what was happening with their sales and trusting their instincts, Lucy and Ryan identified a truly successful formula for their line.

Another example of how observation and intuition can successfully guide your product development comes from Sue Eggen of Giant Dwarf. Sue doesn't have a set process for creating new products and trusts her intuition to tell her when a new product is ready to be born, but she always has a seed of an idea waiting to germinate and grow. She added Fancy Felt supplies to her line when she learned that felt was gaining in popularity. Not only did her overall sales rise, but sourcing the materials was a natural fit since Sue was already using felt in her line of hats and accessories. "Having all of this felt around is inspiration in itself for developing my product line," Sue says.

Branding Your Business

Branding is more than just a logo. It is the overall look and feel of your products and your business, including everything from the way you package and present your products, to the images and color palette you use, to your font selection and descriptive/promotional language, to your sources of inspiration and the subject matter featured in your work.

In addition to his line of rock posters, Jeffrey Everett of El Jefe Design, based in Washington, DC, works with various companies and other organizations to create cohesive brands. Jeff, who has won awards for his efforts, has a solid understanding of how to create a complete package of marketing collateral to clearly define a brand. Several years ago, he produced a promotional mailer for his company that included a small catalog of his prints that looked like a mini art book, incorporating a distinctive color scheme and fonts, as well as his signature *lucha libre* (Mexican wrestler) imagery. Not only was the book a great vehicle for showcasing the variety of design work Jeff produces, but it also highlighted the consistency of brand definition in his work. The mailer, packaged in an envelope that featured the El Jefe logo, further defined the brand by including playful stickers.

Something's Hiding in Here is another great example of a consistent brand that is easily recognizable. Everything about the aesthetic that Shauna Alterio and Stephen Loidolt have created with their Mustaches on a Stick, wooden rings, and cross-stitch yo-yos has been a conscious decision that supports their brand. Even the name Something's Hiding in Here was a deliberate choice. Shauna explains, "What we loved about the name Something's Hiding is that it's broad. When we applied to do our first Renegade show, we didn't know what this business might end up being. So we really wanted to find something that was a little

bit ambiguous and would give us room to make Something's Hiding whatever it wants to become, and it's constantly evolving."

The overall look and feel of Something's Hiding's products is clean, simple, and natural. There is a vintage vibe to their line, and each piece that they lovingly make exudes quality. "We don't want it to always look handmade—we want it to *be* handmade," Shauna says. "So we look for the simplest, most effective way to make the things that we are making. That's not fussy— that's clean. That's definitely a part of our natural aesthetic. . . . We have a palette of colors, we have a palette of materials that we feel somewhat connected to, and that's natural. Over time we have recognized that as long as we don't stray from that, the larger identity works itself out."

Packaging doesn't have to be elaborate to work. Making sure your logo is clear and visible throughout your packaging helps keep your brand easily recognizable.

Keeping a consistent look and feel turns individual products into a cohesive line and emphasizes your brand identity.

Seeing your fonts, colors, and logos laid out in sample forms can help you get a clear idea of how your brand can be viewed.

Defining Your Brand

THROUGH

PHOTOGRAPHY

The images of your products that you use on the web and in printed promotional materials can help align your product line with your brand and make your marketing efforts go the extra mile. Here are some tricks for achieving this:

Feature yourself in your product shots. By doing so, you become your brand. Or does your brand become you? The idea is to align yourself with your products so that when people see shots of your products, they instantly know who made them. This can work especially well if you do a lot of in-person public outreach, whether at craft shows or industry events.

Using yourself as a model in your product shots can also help bring cohesiveness to your line even if you make one-of-a-kind, made-to-order items or use repurposed materials. Sue Eggen provides a great example. Seeing Sue's face in the photos of her Giant Dwarf headbands gives you the sense you are looking at a real handmade item rather than some random headband.

Becky Striepe of Glue and Glitter also appears in her product photos, sporting her "cupcaprons," made from reused fabric, as she prepares food in her kitchen surrounded by vintage Pyrex ware and other nostalgic lovelies.

Infuse your branding into the background of your photos. This might mean creating a backdrop that features your logo or other style elements from your marketing toolbox (your fonts, accent colors, textures, mascots, etc.). It might also mean using models and props to convey the lifestyle your brand represents. Make sure, though, that these branding elements stay in the background so they don't distract from the items you are featuring. Remember, your product, not the background, should be the main focus of the photograph.

If your product line is connected to a particular lifestyle, find ways of evoking that lifestyle in your images. For example, if you make bike messenger bags, photograph your bags on a model riding a bike or posed amid biking gear. Think about the connections between the people and things around you—your family, friends, coworkers, pets, plants—and the products you make. You may be surprised at the simple, brilliant discoveries you'll find. And—who knows?—you might even find a celebrity willing to pose for a product shot.

Play with the lighting. If you make a line of baby doll dresses, use bright, summery light to give your photos an airy feeling. If your products tend toward the dark side—incorporating imagery of skulls or zombies—think of accentuating the shadows in your photos to emphasize the ambience of your brand. But make sure your photographs aren't too dark, or you'll defeat the purpose of the technique. Remember, you want potential customers to be able to see the products you're trying to sell.

This photograph is too dark and the background is too distracting for the product to be noticed.

This photograph is well lit and clear. You know exactly what the product is. Take photographs from different angles to find one that displays your product the best.

This photograph is a good start, but the background is cluttered and customers can't see enough of the scarf itself.

This photograph focuses on just the scarf, and the styling allows customers to envision how to wear it. For more on product photography, see page 80.

Chapter

5

SELLING
ONLINE

Now that you have a clear idea what your business is going to be and what products you are going to produce, it is time to figure out where you can and should sell your wares. After all, if you can't sell your products or services, you don't have much of a business!

One avenue for getting your product into customers' hands is the Internet. Now that the Internet infuses our daily lives, there are more upsides than downsides to selling your products online. Whether you sell through Etsy, another online craft store, or your own website, the Internet opens up a whole world of potential buyers.

There are several reasons you may want to sell online. Having an online presence makes it easy for potential buyers and repeat customers to find you. Say you're selling your super-soft wool scarves at a craft fair, and a shopper is indecisive about buying one. She thinks one of your scarves would make a great gift, but she wants to make sure that the friend she has in mind doesn't already have a scarf like it and isn't allergic to wool. If you have an online shop set up and list the URL on your business cards and marketing materials, it's easy for her to buy from you at a later date. And if she really loves you, then she may bookmark your shop or add it to her "Favorites" section on Etsy or save it as a browser favorite or on a bookmarking site such as Pinterest. Shopper by shopper, you'll be forming a regular customer base.

Another "pro" to having an online store is that it is "open" 24/7, year-round and around the world. You can't possibly travel to each and every craft fair to sell your wares. Plus, the craft fair circuit is seasonal; there are a string of shows in the spring and summer, then in the fall and winter leading up to the holidays, but the January-to-spring stretch can be bone dry. By contrast, your online shop is *always* there.

Your shop can also help you reach an audience you'd otherwise never reach. It's easy for someone in Europe or Asia or Australia to stumble upon your products in an online store—or for someone from the Midwest to buy from you, even if you've never been there. Online stores such as Etsy offer guidance on selling to international buyers and on what to charge for shipping.

An online store is also good to have when you get online press. It gives bloggers and editors an easy way to link to your work— giving readers the opportunity to instantly see (and, hopefully, order!) your product.

There are, however, some downsides to selling online. You may not have enough time to manage your online shop. If, say, you are fulfilling large wholesale orders, or if you're only a part-time crafter who focuses on local craft fairs, you might not have the time to keep up with an online shop. It takes work to sell online: You have to photograph each item, write descriptions for each listing, update listings, and ship things out in a timely fashion whenever a customer buys—not to mention setting aside time to create.

There are also fees to consider. Depending on where you sell and your monthly volume of sales, the amount you spend for online selling might be more than you are willing or can afford to pay. Luckily, there are now plenty of e-commerce solutions that are relatively inexpensive if not free. The pros to online selling definitely outweigh the cons, however, so you should consider adding it to your business if you haven't already.

Online Shops

Here are some options for you to consider when choosing an online shop. Make sure you read the online shop's user agreement and understand the costs involved before signing up with any site. Be sure, too, to consider an online shop's aesthetic before making your choice. Think of how your brand will or won't fit in, and about whether your audience—or ideal audience—is likely to be searching the site.

Etsy

Founded in 2005, Etsy (etsy.com) has become one of the most popular sites among crafters for selling online. According to comScore, a marketing-measurement website, Etsy had 5 million monthly visitors in mid-2011. (Its next-closest competitor, ArtFire, had just 500,000.) Besides offering a place to sell your wares, Etsy provides a community for those selling and buying handmade and vintage. The site's forums are extremely active, and there are special Etsy teams that help promote real-life community all over the world. The *Etsy* blog provides useful advice through its "Etsy Success" series and inspiration through its recurring "Quit Your Day Job" series.

On the most general level, Etsy categorizes items for sale as handmade, vintage, or supplies. Then items are placed in any of thirty-plus categories that range from plants to edibles to "geekery" to accessories to wedding to . . . well, it's a long list! You pay a fee to list each item, and Etsy takes a percentage from the transaction when the item sells.

Etsy has become synonymous with handmade, so just having a modest shop with only a few listed items is worth your  time. Sign-up is easy and takes only minutes. What takes a bit more time and effort is making your shop look good—with beautiful photographs of your items and well-written product descriptions.

ArtFire

Since ArtFire (artfire.com, founded 2008) is not curated, anyone can sell via this e-commerce site. The online shop organizes items for sale in the following six categories: handmade, fine art, craft supplies, vintage, design, and media. ArtFire does not charge fees to list items and does not take money from sales. Its navigation bar offers a number of search options, allowing visitors to look for items that are on sale or for which there is free shipping. A "Buy One Get One" deal is one of the options programmed into the navigation bar to entice shoppers.

Besides being an e-commerce site, ArtFire has forums, a weekly podcast with the CEO and COO, and the *ArtDaily* blog, which features project how-to's and seller profiles.

Cosa Verde

Cosa Verde (cosaverde.com, founded 2009) is a curated site that features eco-friendly goods. It is not technically an e-commerce site, but rather a medium for advertising your goods. When a user clicks on one of your listings, they're transferred to your shop on Etsy, ArtFire, or another online store (or to your own website). Since Cosa Verde is curated, you have to apply to list items there.

Cosa Verde organizes items in the following seven categories: organic, reusable, repurposed, recyclable, conflict-free, cruelty-free, and vegan. There is a monthly fee, which differs depending on whether you choose the basic, standard, or premium subscription level. You receive a credit when you first set up your shop, and you can earn additional credits by referring other sellers to the site and by trading goods for subscription discounts.

Big Cartel

Big Cartel (bigcartel.com, founded 2005) is an e-commerce site that offers sellers various pricing levels. There's no fee per transaction, but you may have to pay a monthly fee, depending on how many products you want to sell through the site. The lowest pricing level is free, but it only allows you to sell five products; the highest level, which costs $29.95 per month as of this writing, allows you to sell hundreds. Big Cartel is customizable, which you may want to take advantage of, depending on your comfort with HTML. The plus side of customization is that you can match the look of your Big Cartel shop to that of your own website and your overall brand.

Shopify

Shopify (shopify.com, founded 2006) is another e-commerce solution with many useful features, including full customization. Shopify's monthly plans range from $29 to $179, depending on how many items you have in your shop and what percentage of the transaction fee you are willing to pay (0 to 2 percent, depending on the plan). With Shopify, you can host your store on your own website or on the Shopify site. The site also offers mobile apps and analytics so you can keep up-to-date with who is shopping on your site and which items are racking up page views. Shopify, which now boasts more than 15,000 shops, has quickly become a popular choice because of its easy-to-understand user interface and mobile options.

Storenvy

Storenvy (storenvy.com, founded 2008) is an online-marketplace-meets-social-shopping experience. It gives buyers the opportunity to follow others who have similar tastes to see what products and stores they are interested in. It also allows buyers to follow stores, so they can receive updates directly from their favorite sellers. As with Big Cartel, the offerings on Storenvy aren't limited to handmade products. Shops on Storenvy are completely customizable, letting you have the same look and feel as your brand (if you are HTML-savvy). It is free to use Storenvy—the only costs the seller incurs are the transaction fees that payment processors such as PayPal charge.

Shopping Carts

Another option to consider is to incorporate a shop or shopping cart directly on your website. The plus side to this is that your online store can be 100 percent personalized. The downside is that it can be frustrating to get the results you want unless you are an experienced HTML wrangler, have techy friends, or hire someone to build your site for you. You need to be technically savvy in order to create a good shop that functions properly and is designed with your brand in mind, but it is a good option for those who have the time to fiddle with code and want to take a truly DIY approach to building their own online store.

For shopping cart platforms, Zen Cart (zen-cart.com), osCommerce (oscommerce.com), Magento (magentocommerce.com), PrestaShop (prestashop.com), and CubeCart (cubecart.com) all provide good options. Some are open-source platforms and therefore free to use, while others charge fees for their use.

Curated Online Shops

Once you have a product line developed and feel you have a strong brand, you might want to consider applying to sell your work in a curated online shop. Many buyers of handmade goods prefer curated shops because they offer high-quality merchandise and because each curated shop represents a certain kind of taste. Sites like Etsy and ArtFire, which are not curated, offer thousands of products catering to many different tastes, so it may be difficult for buyers to find things they like on such sites. But if a customer knows that their taste is similar to, say, that of the curators of Buyolympia, then they'll go to that online store expecting to lust after many of the products on offer.

As a seller, you'll have to apply to each curated store separately, and follow each store's specific application guidelines. As with any situation in which your work is being "juried," there is no guarantee you will be chosen. You present your best work so that the jury—in this case the online store's owners—can get a good sense of who you are and what you can do. You may be asked to include a bio or product descriptions with your application. As in any juried competition, the quality of the photos you submit can make or break your chances of being selected, so make sure your photos are beautiful.

With so many curated stores to choose from, you might find yourself at a loss trying to decide which ones to apply to. The best thing to do is to evaluate the shop's online traffic and its aesthetic and to find out how many artists/crafters it normally stocks. This information will help you find a shop that fits your brand. Feel free to apply to more than one if you think you'll have the time to keep up with selling on several sites.

Sara Selepouchin of Girls Can Tell sells her totes, prints, and other products on Etsy and the curated store Supermarket, as well as on her own online shop, hosted by Big Cartel. She says, "I see more sales on a regular basis through Etsy. They've been making so many improvements on the seller's side, it's been amazing how many seller tools they've released. They've always had such strong traffic, and when people think of 'handmade,' they automatically think of Etsy. Having an Etsy shop is sort of the standard now. I don't understand people who make things by hand and don't have an Etsy shop, just because it's so easy. But at the same time I've always been a firm believer in not putting all of your eggs in one basket. I knew that in order to grow my brand, I couldn't only have an Etsy shop."

A Wholesale Option: Trunkt

Trunkt (trunkt.com, founded 2008) is a website focused solely on connecting wholesale buyers and sellers. Since Trunkt is not an e-commerce site, there is no shopping cart, and there's no way to earn money via the site itself. Trunkt leaves the checkout and payment entirely up to you and the buyer. It gives sellers a place to showcase wholesale items all in one place, as well as tools for managing their wholesale business.

Think of it as a place to which you can point prospective wholesale buyers anytime you have a wholesale inquiry.

Anyone who is ready to accept wholesale orders can use Trunkt. There is a monthly fee after you sign up, but there are no commissions or charges for product listings. To gain access to a seller's wholesale prices on Trunkt, prospective buyers must enter their website name, retail type, and resale ID or federal tax ID.

Popular Curated Online Stores

Many curated stores now operate online. Here are a few of the most popular:

- **Buyolympia (buyolympia.com).** The original online shop for handmade goods, Buyolympia continues to stay true to its roots by offering selected quality items from indie artists and crafters.
- **Craftland (craftlandshow.com).** Craftland offers a small selection from its retail shop, including illustrations, jewelry, notebooks, tote bags, and more.
- **Renegade Handmade (renegadehandmade.com).** Renegade's online shop offers a wide selection of handmade goods from the same artists and crafters found in its retail space.
- **Shana Logic (shanalogic.com).** The Shana Logic website has an appealingly clean and modern look.
- **Supermarket (supermarkethq.com).** Supermarket offers a wide range of handmade items. The site features individual designers and crafters and their collections.

Setting Up Your Online Shop

When setting up your online shop, keep the buyer in mind. Remember that when customers visit your shop, they will be relying solely on your photography and item descriptions to understand what they are buying. To improve your chances of closing a sale, you've got to make your photography and descriptions enticing.

When writing item descriptions, go in depth without going overboard—you're not writing a novel! Be detailed yet concise. Most important, don't skimp on the important stuff, like the story behind your product. Did you source your materials by upcycling found objects? Are you using only eco-friendly materials? Did you start making your product for a particular reason that others can connect with? All these specifics are part of your brand and should be expressed in your online shop.

Providing clear and appealing photographs of your products is, if anything, even more important. Snappy product names and detailed item descriptions are essential to being a successful seller, but the images are the first thing a potential customer will see—so make sure they're beautiful.

Put yourself in the customer's shoes. There are more than 400,000 shops on Etsy alone, and when a customer browses through hundreds of listings, everything starts to blend together. So how will you distinguish yourself from the next seller? Partly through professional-looking photographs. If the product shots are enticing, your chances of securing a sale greatly increase.

Product Photography Basics

If you are just starting out with product photography, there are a few things to keep in mind. First, an expensive, top-of-the-line camera is not necessary. With a simple point-and-shoot digital camera in the $300 range, you can achieve professional-looking photos. If you follow key photography techniques such as using natural light, focusing on your product, and editing properly, you'll get great-looking photos with a lower-end camera. Whatever camera you find yourself working with, do make sure to read the manual and to familiarize yourself with all the features before setting up your product shots.

How do you go about finding the camera that's best for you? Leethal's Lee Meredith suggests browsing Flickr for user groups and photo tags with the camera's name. She explains: "If you make jewelry, look for photos of small things, to be sure the macro focus is great; if you shoot colorful products, make sure the colors pop and look accurate and balanced. Also, be sure to look at photos by lots of different users—if one person's photos look fabulous, but most others are dull or ugly, then that first person might just be excellent at Photoshop, and the camera might be terrible."

If you have more money to spend and a real interest in learning about digital photography, Lee suggests that you consider buying a digital single-lens reflex (DSLR) camera, which will give you more control. Depending on what you're shooting, however, you may not be able to get the quality of photos you want out of a DSLR without

also buying another lens, since the kit lenses that come with DSLRs are not suited to product photography. Lenses are expensive, so you'll be adding another couple of hundred dollars to your equipment cost. You may need a macro lens, a micro lens, or possibly a lens with a huge aperture (which means a small f/number—f/1.4 or f/1.8) to let in extra light and narrow the depth of field (to blur out background).

Lighting Your Photos

The way you light your product photos is as important as the camera you have. Just look at the photographs on pages 70 and 71. First rule: Shut off your flash. Always make sure that the light is ample enough that your photos will be clear, bright, and focused directly on the item you are selling. If you have enough light, problems like unfocused pictures due to shaky hands will be eliminated.

The best light is natural, indirect (or diffused) light from the sun, so try taking photos in a room that gets plenty of sunlight. If the light is too direct, hang sheer curtains on the windows to diffuse the sunlight coming through.

Unfortunately, not every online seller has a sunlit room or the time to schedule photo shoots on sunny days. But there are still ways to produce professional-looking photographs in the absence of natural light. One is to build a light box. A light box is just what it sounds like—a box with holes in its sides that allow diffused light to enter. You don't have to invest in expensive equipment for this. Los Angeles–based photographer Ben High built his first light box out of a discarded box he found in a parking garage. He cut big squares out of each side and taped tracing paper over them to evenly diffuse the light, then used his homemade box to take photographs of jewelry.

When photographing products indoors under artificial light, think about the light source you're using. Fluorescent bulbs give off a cool, bluish hue, whereas "white" incandescent lightbulbs emit a warmer, more yellow light. You can use clear lightbulbs if you want to prevent your photos from taking on a certain color. But whichever kind of bulb you decide to use, stick to just that one type. This will help ensure that your photos have a bright, clear appearance.

A Do-It-Yourself Light Box

You'll need the following tools and materials:

- medium-size cardboard box (approximately 24" × 24" × 24" [61cm x 61cm x 61cm])
- ruler
- pencil
- scissors
- box cutter
- white tissue paper
- masking tape
- plain white paper (copy paper will suffice)

First, cut the flaps off the top of the box. Then measure and mark off a large square (or rectangle, if your box isn't a perfect cube) on each of two opposite sides of the box, leaving a one-inch border along all four edges. Cut out the two squares.

Now cut two pieces of tissue paper into squares half an inch wider and longer than the square holes you cut. Tape the tissue-paper squares over the holes, trimming off excess if necessary. Line the whole interior of the box except for the tissue paper–covered holes with the white paper, carefully taping it in place.

Your light box is now ready to use! Set it under or near a window or use it outside in sunlight. You can also use the light box inside with an artificial light source.

Background and Product Display

As we discussed in the section on branding in chapter 4, you should think about the background of your product photos before you start shooting. Your photos' purpose is to give potential buyers the chance to see your handmade items—not a cluttered house or yard! Whatever you decide, make sure the background is not a distraction. If you don't have anything particular in mind, stick with a plain background, which can be achieved with an ironed white sheet or large white-paper backdrop.

Before shooting, you'll also need to think about how your products will be displayed. If the item is small and flat (like a ring), prop it on something so the customer will see all of it and not just one side. Take photos of the item from a few different angles, and don't be afraid of close-up shots.

If your products are clothes or accessories, find a willing friend to be your model instead of using a mannequin. This lets buyers see the product "in action" and helps them picture themselves wearing it.

Get display ideas by browsing online to see how other sellers are presenting similar items. Just make sure your photos are bright, clear, and sharply detailed. No matter how you choose to display an item, make sure the *product* is the picture's focus.

Editing Your Photos

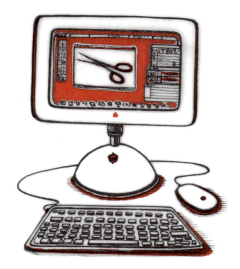

After you have taken your product shots, you'll need to edit your photos for use in your online store. You'll probably have to crop and resize images, and also perhaps to adjust for color balance, sharpness, and brightness/contrast. Your camera might have come with photo editing software; if not, you'll have to explore other options. The following are a few of the photo editing software programs now available. Some you have to pay for; others are free:

- Aviary (free; aviary.com)
- Gimp (free; gimp.org)
- IrfanView (free; irfanview.com)
- Photoshop (pay; photoshop.com)
- Photoshop Elements (pay; adobe.com/products/photoshopel)

- Picnik (free, pay for upgrade; picnik.com)
- pixlr (free; pixlr.com)
- PIXresizer (free; pixresizer.en.softonic.com)

The specifics of using editing features such as brightness/contrast and levels/curves depend on the editing program. Leethal's Lee Meredith says she usually tries the automatic enhancement functions—auto levels, auto color balance, and auto brightness—first. If those don't satisfy her, she'll do further manual adjustments as needed—usually to the levels and then to the curves to add extra contrast. If you can't decide what level of brightness/contrast is best for your product shot, Lee advises you to find similar images online that look great and to compare your in-progress shots to those photos while editing, trying your best to match their brightness/contrast setting.

When cropping, trim the photo so that the product is up close and centered. But don't crop *too* up close. You want to leave enough background in the image to give the product some context. Make sure you crop before you do any resizing.

Be aware that different online stores have different sizing and formatting requirements. For Etsy, you'll want to crop the image to 1,000 pixels wide. A horizontal (landscape) format is recommended over a vertical (portrait) format because of how photos get automatically cropped by Etsy in the thumbnail view. Your online store's FAQ page may answer questions you have about image size and format, or there may be a thread in one of the store's forums offering specific guidelines.

> *Be aware that different online stores have different sizing and formatting requirements.*

Using Analytics to Gauge Your Online Shop's Success

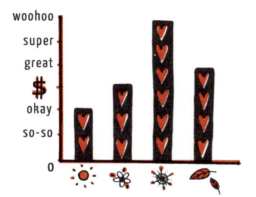

Gauging the success of your online store is subjective. It has to be based on your own particular reasons for selling online and what you want and need to get out of it. Your idea of success won't necessarily match someone else's. Not everyone can and should be Emily Martin, of the Black Apple, who has racked up over 35,000 sales on Etsy alone with her illustrations, art, and paper goods. That said, there is a concrete way to measure how well you are doing: through the data you can collect via Google Analytics.

No matter what type or types of web presence you decide to set up—website, blog, Etsy shop, or whatever—it is a good idea also to install Google Analytics. This free tool from Google can give you powerful insight into how people find your site, how long people stay on your site, and what pages or posts are most popular. Analytics can help you track trends in your web traffic—even letting you know, for example, whether that blog ad you bought drove traffic to your site and was worth the money you paid to run it.

Setting up Analytics is pretty simple. Anyone with a Google account can sign up, and instructions can be found in Google Help. Once you have Analytics set up, you can start to explore. Some of the specific measurements Analytics provides include the following:

- **Visitors.** Who is visiting your shop, and when?
- **Map overlay.** Where in the world do your visitors come from?
- **Bounce rate.** What percentage of your visitors view only one page and then leave?
- **Page views versus unique page views.** How many times is each page viewed—and how many of those views are by unique (i.e., different) visitors?

- **How people find your shop.** Do they find it through search engines (Google, Bing, Yahoo! Search, etc.), through your online store's search function, or some other route?

Analytics is really best for getting a bird's-eye view of your traffic and sales. Pay attention to the highs and lows that are mapped out for you; then try to find out why these highs and lows occurred: Did you see an increase in traffic or sales during the days following a craft fair?

Did you see an uptick after your business got mentioned on a popular blog? (And did visitors come to your shop by clicking on a link in that blog?) Those are just a few examples of what you can see and do with Analytics.

A word of caution, however: While all these data are helpful, obsessing over the minute details that Analytics offers isn't productive. Use it sparingly, looking at the data each month or quarter rather than tracking them day by day (or hour by hour!). You have more important things to do.

I've found that 40 percent of my Etsy shop traffic comes from blogs, which was revealed in Google Analytics.

—SUE EGGAN of Giant Dwarf

Using Analytics to Boost Sales

The data collected by Google Analytics on visits to your online shop can help you measure your return on investment (ROI), better understand your customer base, and increase your sales. Here are some simple ways to use these data:

1. **Analyze the average visit.** What pages do your visitors tend to leave on? Go to those pages and see what might be causing them to leave. A bad photo? A poor item description?
2. **Work on lowering your bounce rate.** To do this, encourage your visitors to check out your main shop profile or another item or section in your online shop.
3. **Keep tabs on your inbound links.** Danielle Maveal, Etsy's seller education coordinator says, "I would *always* keep an eye on inbound links. Who's blogging about you? And always, always send a thank-you e-mail to the blogger, no matter how big or small."
4. **Know where your shoppers live.** This might mean you should consider international shipping if you don't already offer it. Danielle says, "I see a lot of new sellers only shipping within the United States. What if they checked out where their visitors were coming from and found out they actually are turning away a lot of Canadians?"

Chapter

6

SELLING AT CRAFT FAIRS

C raft fairs are an essential part of the indie craft scene. Many successful crafty business owners count craft shows as a helpful stepping-stone for their business. Sue Eggen of Giant Dwarf is a huge advocate of craft shows. She's participated in indie craft shows since 2003 and still tries to do as many as possible. She's found that letting customers look at real, tangible objects gives them a more powerful shopping experience than shopping online and helps establish a stronger connection between her products and potential buyers. Sue also finds that representing her brand in person inherently reinforces the noncorporate attitude shared by many crafters and handmade shoppers.

Craft shows provide a revenue stream for your business both from the immediate infusion of cash derived from sales during the show and from postevent customer follow-up. But how do you know whether you should do a particular craft fair or whether you should even try selling in person at all? There are several factors to take into consideration. One factor is the expense of showing at a fair—not just the expense of producing the products you'll see there, but all the associated expenses, including application fees, booth fees, and travel expenses. Then there's the physical activity involved—hauling your stuff, setting up displays, and just having to stand and smile and talk all day long, all the while remaining friendly to the shoppers that come by your booth.

Face-to-Face Selling

Meeting customers face-to-face is perhaps the greatest benefit that craft show participation offers. Not only do shoppers get to touch your products but they also get to see you and your personality on display. Folks who shop at craft shows tend to want a personal connection with the stuff they buy, and the face-to-face interaction allows you to help customers make connections not afforded by the Internet. As Sue Eggen puts it, "You can feel the product. You can try the product on. You can look at who the artist is and see why they're doing it. You can just tell that the heart and soul of the artist is in their work, as compared to seeing it online."

Besides just meeting your customers in person, you'll have the opportunity to test out new products and marketing tactics. Other selling experiences can't match the "laboratory environment" craft fairs offer. Are you trying to launch a new line but not certain which styles or color combinations will be winners? At a show you can solicit immediate feedback and learn what people do or don't like. This feedback can inspire new products or even the launch of an entirely new line. Rhonda and Elijah Wyman of Figs & Ginger experienced this when they sold out of their first Nestling Birds necklaces at the first-ever *Bust* Craftacular. They quickly figured out who their market was and what types of products they would buy. Before that fair, they'd had only limited success selling Rhonda's art jewelry, but when they sold out of the Nestling Birds necklaces, they developed a line of woodland-creature jewelry, which continues to grow.

Besides letting you sell your wares and, hopefully, turn a profit, craft fairs also provide a great networking opportunity. A show might include anywhere from fifty to two hundred vendors, which means you'll be among a good number of your peers.

Face-to-face interaction isn't for everybody, though. If you are super shy, and the thought of having conversations about your products and completing sales in person makes you want to cry, you'll have to find a solution to that problem before you start to do shows. It's important to overcome such fears if they hold you back from advancing your business, but don't beat yourself up if you're not ready yet. It may take some time. You just have to remember to own your awesome.

Dealing with the Weather

Outdoor markets are subject to the whims of Mother Nature no matter the season. For this reason, selling at an outdoor show can be risky and tiring. Many crafters have melted through two-day summer shows with lethargic shoppers only to schlep their goods to the next fair and experience thunderstorms and product-damaging rain. When the weather cooperates, outdoor shows provide a fantastic atmosphere for handmade shopping, but when it doesn't, you'll have to hustle to get out the plastic sheeting and check that your tent is properly anchored. So consult the *Farmers' Almanac* and hope for the best!

Craft Fair Dos and Don'ts

Do

- ☐ Smile and greet shoppers.
- ☐ Share the story behind your company and products.
- ☐ Keep your focus on the show and enjoy the break from day-to-day operations.
- ☐ Consider demonstrating your process.

Don't

- ☐ Ignore people, cross your arms, or frown.
- ☐ Assume people entering your booth are familiar with your company or process.
- ☐ Work on other business management projects.
- ☐ Leave your booth for extended periods of time without a knowledgeable helper to stay behind.

Planning for a Fair

To make sure you are adequately prepared for a fair, make an effort to plan carefully. Create a timeline with deadlines and a checklist of expenses. Be sure to note the following:

- Date(s) of the show
- Application deadlines, requirements, and fees
- Deadlines for rentals and other vendor services
- When you should book your transportation and lodging
- When to order necessary materials and supplies
- A production timeline with daily/weekly goals and projected completion date
- When you should ship your products

Your timeline/checklist should also include marketing plans—materials to be designed, items to be ordered, and social-media postings and e-mail blasts before, during, and after the show.

Craft fairs are seasonal, tending to clump together in the summer and then again around the holidays. Plan for this, and make sure that a holiday show—when people are in a gift-buying mood, and attendance and sales increase—is on your to-do list.

Choosing the Right Show for You

There are several different types of shows you can pick and choose from: smaller and larger shows, juried and nonjuried shows, and shows catering to different audiences. From traditional shows, like the American Craft Council Show, to indie shows with an edge, like Crafty Bastards Arts & Crafts Fair, there's something out there to fit every crafter's brand.

What's the Fair's Size?

The number and types of vendors and the fair's setup determine the look and feel of the event. Shows like Baltimore's Pile of Craft and Holiday Heap have under a hundred vendors and are run by members of the local craft community. The relatively small number of vendors can be an advantage, as there is less competition. But fewer vendors means fewer crafters promoting the show, so beware of small shows that are poorly promoted by the organizers.

Larger indie craft fairs like Crafty Wonderland, in Portland, Oregon; Crafty Bastards, in Washington, DC; and the several Renegade Craft Fairs (which are now multiday events in several cities across the country and in London) have more than one hundred vendors and draw tens of thousands of shoppers.

Indie craft shows began in the pre-Etsy era, meeting the need for marketplaces with an aesthetic that would attract young buyers. As the handmade movement grew, so did the popularity of indie craft fairs. Websites like Hellocraft.com, Etsy.com, Craftzine.com, Indiefixx.com, and Indiecraftshows.com are all good resources for researching indie craft shows to see which ones may be the right fit for you.

Traditional shows like the American Craft Council Show and the One of a Kind shows usually take place at large convention centers and offer equipment rentals that facilitate a professional-looking retail setting. These, too, are multiday shows with hundreds of vendors and thousands of attendees. The demographic for these shows trends older, so cussword-filled cross-stitch or plush monsters might not fly, whereas simple lined leather bags or utilitarian pottery without ironic decoration might be perfect. If you do screen printing, note that these shows usually don't accept this medium. All items for sale must be wholly handmade.

If you're just starting out, it might not be the best choice to sign up for a multi-day show with thousands of attendees. Getting your feet wet with a smaller-scale show will give you a better chance to test, observe, and tinker with this style of selling.

What's the Audience Like?

Knowing what a craft fair's audience is like and how closely it matches your target audience can also help you select the right fair. Do some online research and talk to crafty friends to find shows that make sense for you.

Tina Seamonster's first craft fair was at a VFW hall—not the best venue for her edgy product line. She sold only one fishing-lure necklace and endured more than one disparaging remark about her work. Needless to say it was a disappointing experience. But later that year, Tina found out about the Crafty Bastards Arts & Crafts Fair. Putting aside the fear she'd developed because of her first experience of selling in person, she decided to apply. Not only did she get into the show, but she almost sold out of all of her wares that day. As Tina

wrote on the *Washington City Paper*'s *Cut the Craft* blog, "What is totally rad about getting into a juried indie craft fair is that odds are at least one person is going to think your stuff is amazing. And if it is a good day, more than one. Maybe ten or fifty or one hundred people will totally love what you do."

Is the Fair Juried or Unjuried?

Juried shows have the advantage of being curated, so the vendors are all likely to be of a certain caliber and to mesh well together. Juried shows can be a challenge to break into, and applying to one carries the possibility of rejection. Unjuried shows give everyone a chance, which is some-times all a craft business needs to get a jump start. But since everyone gets in, there's no telling what sort of quality or aesthetics will be represented at the show, which can make it difficult to attract a mass of shoppers.

Applying to Juried Fairs

To be successful when applying to a juried craft fair, do these three things: follow instructions, write clear and concise product descriptions, and provide good product images.

Following instructions means making sure you provide *everything* the application asks for in the amounts and format requested, which vary from show to show. Before you start the application, carefully read the instructions and make a checklist to be sure you haven't left anything out when you hit Submit.

Clear and concise product descriptions will help the jury understand the connection between you, your products, and your brand. Highlight the handmade nature of your line. (Do you make your own jewelry findings? Screen-print your shirts?) But make every word count.

Good product images are essential. On the *Washington City Paper*'s *Cut the Craft* blog, Tina Seamonster offers these tips on photos: First, she advises you to "submit bright, clear photos of your work! Judges look at hundreds if not thousands of photos when jurying a show. Not only do you want your work to stand out, you don't want to contribute to their eye strain!" Second, she says that you should "show variety in your work. If you make hand-knit scarves as well as kitten booties and iMac cozies, send in a photo of each so the jurors can see the breadth of your work." And third, Tina recommends "showing your work in action. If you make pottery, take a photo of someone enjoying a steaming cup of cocoa in a hand-thrown mug, or if you make pillows, take shots of them on a couch or with your cat napping on them. It gives the viewer context." Finally, Tina suggests injecting "your personality and style and vision into your photos."

In other words, be true to your brand, and make sure every aspect of the application shows what you and your business are about.

Designing Your Space

Once you have found the perfect craft fair for you and have been accepted, you have to think about your booth. Good booth layout and design make it easy for shoppers to quickly survey your products and establish a connection between your product line and brand. There are many ways to do this, and the right setup should be unique to you.

Do some research by going to shows and festivals to look at the variety of booth designs and product displays and to experience them *as a shopper*. As you walk around, take note of the elements that catch your eye. Don't be afraid to compliment the crafters on their setups or to ask questions. Many will be happy to geek out over their displays. (But don't be discouraged if some are unwilling to share their insights. After all, they may have spent years perfecting their setups and have every right to keep their hard-won knowledge to themselves.)

The Internet is an endless resource for booth and product display ideas. Pinterest is a great place to see and collect visual ideas. On the *Etsy* blog, Danielle Maveal recommends the "Show Me Your Booths" Flickr group and notes that retail shops and their catalogs are also good sources for inspiration, particularly when the company sells the same category of goods as you.

The best booth displays seamlessly weave the character of the company's brand into all their elements without overwhelming shoppers with the design. For example, Caitlin Phillips of Rebound Designs reinforces her brand by hanging a paper garland cut from old books in her craft fair booths, subtly complementing her line of book purses and paperback wallets.

Seek out fixtures and accessories that correspond to the look and feel of your brand. If your brand is clean and modern, IKEA probably has the products for you. If your look is more rustic or shabby chic, thrift stores, vintage shops, and estate sales may be your best resources. Generally speaking, stores that cater to small-space living and organization are good sources for fixtures and accessories. Craigslist, yard sales, and flea markets are also great sources. Keep an eye out for opportunities like going-out-of-business sales and prop sales from theatrical companies, too.

Understanding Craft Fair Requirements

Different shows require different levels of investment when it comes to setup and display, so be sure you understand and are okay with the requirements before signing your vendor agreement. For example, many outdoor indie shows suggest that you rent an optional pop-up tent, while other festivals require tents set up by festival staff and include the tent rental in the vendor fee.

Requirements likewise vary for indoor shows. Indoor indie craft shows often give you space for a couple of tables or clothing racks, while large trade, wholesale, and traditional craft shows often require a higher level of investment for constructed stalls offering a more defined space. They also offer an array of services such as lighting, product-stand rentals, and pipe and drape packages. A word of caution to novices: At big shows, expenses associated with rentals can add up quickly. Be sure you understand your needs, and budget wisely. Because of a miscalculation on the amount of booth space and number of tables needed, Hello Craft once spent an extra $75 per day for a table rental at a three-day show. Ouch.

If you participate in outdoor craft shows, a tent or other type of cover can make a world of difference. Not only does the tent help you define your space and set it physically apart from the booths around you, it

also provides much-needed protective cover in case of burning sun or drenching rain.

Customizing Your Layout

Imagine that you are a customer entering your booth for the first time. What fixtures and accessories will enhance the customer's shopping experience? If you do a lot of shows, you may want to have a setup for outdoor spring shows that is completely different from the setup you use for indoor holiday shows. Or, you may want to design your booth in a way that is versatile enough to work in just about any environment. That's what Caitlin Phillips of Rebound Designs has done: she always uses the same backdrop for displaying her line of book purses, but she adds and removes various fixtures like bookshelves or small tables to suit her needs at different shows.

Some kinds of products require specific fixtures. If you sell hats or jewelry, people should be able to try them on, so make sure you have a mirror or two. If you sell dresses, skirts, and tops, it probably makes sense to construct some sort of dressing room. A camping shower, a curtain, or even just a large piece of fabric pinned across a corner of your booth can serve as a utilitarian dressing room.

Figure out how to make it easy for customers to survey your booth and see all the items you are offering. This usually means getting some of your products up off the table. Think about using the floor, arranging things at different heights across a table, or hanging things across the back or along the sides of your booth. Your booth lives in 3-D, and so should your products.

Getting Noticed

If you're of average height and you've ever been in the middle of a crowded craft fair, you've undoubtedly had the frustrating experience of trying to figure out where you are and what booth you're next to. You desperately search for the names of vendors, until at last you see a booth that has its signage prominently and conveniently displayed on the *outside* of the booth at a height that can be seen above the crowd. Take a lesson from that experience. Get noticed by hanging a sign at a height that's visible and that reflects the look and feel of you and your products.

Becky Striepe of Glue and Glitter has a handmade banner featuring a collage of vintage and upcycled fabric, like the fabric she uses in her products. Rachel Bone of Red Prairie Press displays a simple fabric

Give Good Booth

The following are great examples of innovative booth displays that highlight the crafter's brand and entice potential customers into buying.

Something's Hiding in Here. Shauna Alterio and Stephen Loidolt combine muted color and clean design to create a space that captures the mood of the products they are selling at a given show. Whether they use a wooden bakery case painted in a cheerful blue palette and filled with colorful goodies or a single jewelry case displaying wooden pieces set against a woodland backdrop, their booth design is always tailored to mirror their product line and enhance the way the line is viewed.

Tugboat Printshop. Paul Roden and Valerie Lueth's display has evolved over the years from a simple table lined with prints into a very professional-looking "pop-up" gallery. The unit folds out to give shoppers the impression they are viewing work on a gallery wall, which nudges them toward comprehending the level of skill and amount of work that go into each of Tugboat's intricately hand-carved woodblock prints. This helps prepare the shopper for the limited-edition prints' cost, which might seem rather expensive compared with the jewelry, cards, or screen-printed shirts in the next booth over. Tugboat's professional-looking setup provides the proper context for viewing—and encouraging shoppers to buy—their prints.

Biggs and Featherbelle. Kelly and Kasey Evick's soap is clean and green, and that aesthetic is perfectly mirrored in their booth setup. They display a minimal amount of product and keep additional stock neatly stored away and out of sight. Astroturf, vases, and potted plants (both real and fake), enhance the clean-and-green feel of the booth. By integrating the colorful dots used on their product packaging into their booth's table covers and signage, they drive home the connection between their products and their brand, increasing their brand recognition.

banner across the top of her booth, flanked by items from her line of screen-printed apparel. Joshua Betz of Gnome Enterprises uses bunting made of felt leaves and cardboard letters that wraps around two sides of a tent, providing optimal viewing.

Packaging and Pricing

You'll lose customers if you fail to provide the information they need to make a purchase. Think of your booth as a crafty buffet full of somewhat mysterious but potentially delicious items waiting to be consumed. Point out some of your most popular items to help steer shoppers in their direction, while using well-placed info cards, images, and price tags to deepen customers' understanding of your products and to let them know the cost.

If you use top-dollar supplies to create your products, it may not be obvious to a shopper who is unfamiliar with your brand or with the handmade community. By sharing a bit of your knowledge and explaining your material choices on the price tags or signage, you may increase shoppers' willingness to spend more, particularly if their values are reflected in your material choices. As part of her booth setup, Erica Gordon of Steel Toe Studios includes a digital slideshow of her forging and welding metal. Those images of a petite woman using heat and water to manipulate metal set against her polished and well-presented product line instantly enhance shoppers' understanding of the connection between the woman at the register and the products in the booth.

Always consider your products' medium and whether the show's environment might damage your products. For example, if you sell art prints or stationery, use packaging that will protect them against the elements and against being soiled. You don't want your paper goods to be ruined by heat or humidity—or to get dirty from being picked up one too many times by grubby hands.

Also think about offering a lower price on the products you sell at shows. This can be a tipping point for someone who's been stalking your online shop, and it encourages people to buy more.

Dealing with Problems

If there's a problem, handle it professionally. Remember to remain calm and courteous. If you encounter an unhappy customer, your best bet is to respond with a huge smile, a sense of humor, and thick skin. Baseless complaints, innocent misunderstandings, and theft are just some of the things that may go wrong. Don't get defensive; use the opportunity to fix the problem or educate customers about their misconceptions. If someone returns a defective product—a handbag with a broken snap, a chipped bowl—immediately apologize and offer to replace the item or fix the problem.

Theft sucks, but it happens. Do your best to keep your products secure, and be aware of who is in your booth and what they are checking out. Should you fall victim to a shoplifter, alert the show organizers, as you may be able to describe or identify a suspect. If the loss is hefty enough, file a police report for insurance purposes or so you can document the loss for tax purposes.

Selling Tips

- Say hello and smile whenever someone enters your booth.
- Ask customers if they are familiar with the materials/process used in items they are looking at.
- Encourage them to ask questions.
- Reorganize or futz with products near shoppers so it is easy to see what catches their interest and to start a conversation.
- Offer specific compliments about things customers are wearing—but only if the compliments are sincere!
- Think about ways to engage customers when they walk by your booth, enter, are about to leave, or seem interested in buying a specific item.

Organizing Your Own Craft Fair

Ready to try organizing your own craft show? Curating and producing a show and sale of your favorite handmade goods can be a very satisfying experience and is a great way to support the handmade community. Before you dive in, though, you'll have to outline the various aspects of your event and formulate a strategic plan. Here are some preliminary questions you'll have to ask yourself:

What Will the Show's Size and Scope Be?

Do you want to produce a small trunk sale on a weekday evening, or would you rather produce a multiday event with hundreds of vendors? Carefully consider your resources and your capacity for undertaking the project while balancing your existing responsibilities. Producing a show like Crafty Bastards, a one-day event with hundreds of vendors and over 30,000 shoppers, requires several months of planning to pull together the many partners, permits, and components of the festival. If the inspiration for producing your own show comes from the desire to create the ideal market for selling your handmade goods, a smaller-scale show is the way to go. If your dream is to impact your community and support handmade artists, go for a big show or one that happens on a frequent basis.

How Much Support Will You Have?

While it's not absolutely necessary, having a partner in crime or core group of committed helpers to support the endeavor can make the show more feasible and the process more enjoyable. More hands mean you can spread the work out, and it will take less time to accomplish all the tasks needed to organize a show.

What About the Venue?

Think about your dream list of vendors and the shoppers they are likely to attract, and then seek out venues appropriate for your target audience. The more flexible a space is, the more easily you can adapt it to suit your needs, but make sure it is somewhere shoppers are likely to go. If your customers tend to live, work, and play near a city center, an affordable reception hall in the outer 'burbs doesn't make sense—whereas a downtown café, club, or park probably does. Other potentially affordable options include conveniently located churches, schools, community centers, and parking lots.

When Will the Show Be Held?

Always try to set and announce your event date as early as possible. Be sure to check what other popular shows are happening around the time that you are planning yours and avoid dates that compete with other craft shows.

How Will You Attract Vendors?

There are two basic ways to attract vendors: through invitation or by issuing a call for applications. Invitations work well for small shows, while larger shows often require an application process.

Consider the potential volume of applications and your data management needs when setting up your application process and determining how the vendors will be selected. Online form-building services like Google Docs and Wufoo can help you collect and manage data. Reviewing and accepting vendors on a rolling basis until all vendor slots are full is one option; another is to set an application deadline, after which you'll review all entries and notify applicants of their status. Select your jurors from the community—people you know who are interested in arts and crafts—and make sure they all understand the qualities you are looking for from vendors and the criteria for acceptance.

Once you've selected the vendors, you'll need to get them to sign agreements and to pay vendor fees. If you are going to offer equipment rentals, it's easiest to have participants reserve and pay for the rentals when they submit their signed contracts and booth fees. You'll also want to cover your butt with a "holds harmless" clause that states that you are not liable for the myriad things that could possibly go wrong during the fair, and you'll want to outline your expectations for show participation in your vendor agreement. You may wish to consult with a lawyer when drawing up this contract.

How Will You Promote the Event?

To promote your event effectively, you'll want a stand-alone web presence for your fair. Whether that's a highly involved website or a simple Facebook invite is up to you. Help promote your fair via social media, blogs, and print outreach, including advertisements. Follow the same basic marketing principles found in chapter 8. If possible, feature vendors and images of their work on your show's website and have press info available.

Don't forget that your vendors are running businesses and need to promote themselves, too. This can amplify your marketing message. Provide vendors with promotional materials like press releases, show logos, and graphics to make it easy for them to promote their show participation to their customer base and fans. Seek out media sponsors and partnerships to help get your ads in front of their audiences.

Event Logistics

Event logistics are not very sexy, but they are oh so important! They break down into what you'll have to do *before* the event (the organizing stage) and what you'll do during the event itself (the execution). Here are some considerations:

Organize

Will you need permits? What kind—and what are the fees associated with them? Do you need to coordinate with other companies or agencies? Do you have a signed agreement with the venue, and do the venue's managers understand the event's requirements? Do you need security? What about event insurance? Is that covered under your venue agreement, or do you need to acquire it separately? What about your budget? Are you projecting a profit or loss? You'll need to map the space, assign booth placements, and communicate all the deadlines and expectations to your vendors so they know when and where to show up.

And here are some other questions you'll need to answer: Will you charge admission to customers? If so, how will you handle ticket sales? Do you need a program? If so, what's the timeline for getting it printed? Will you need extra hands during the event? How will you go about recruiting volunteers? What about taxes? The rules for taxes vary from state to state, so be sure to check with your local agency.

Execute

You are near the finish line, but you need to get through the event first. Plan to be the first person to arrive and the last person to leave. Onsite execution can be physically and mentally exhausting, so prepare by getting enough sleep and eating healthily during the days leading up to the show, and by setting specific goals for the day.

Everyone attending your event is a potential customer, so make sure they're treated accordingly. Be ready to resolve vendor conflicts, and don't forget to capture the event with photos and videos, to collect e-mail addresses, and to thank vendors and attendees for supporting the event. After the event, send out a vendor survey to get feedback on what worked and what could be improved. Then relax and pat yourself on the back for a job well done.

Craft Fair
SURVIVAL KIT

Besides having a "booth babe" (a friend or volunteer to help you out), here are some other necessities you'll want to have with you in the booth to make your sales go more smoothly and to get you through the craft fair day:

- [ ] Bottled water
- [ ] Change
- [ ] Cash box
- [ ] Credit card reader
- [ ] "Knuckle buster" and credit card slips
- [ ] Calculator
- [ ] Cell phone (a smartphone is best)
- [ ] Branded shopping bags
- [ ] Business cards
- [ ] Promo cards offering online discounts
- [ ] Office supplies (pens, markers, tape, paper clips, rubber bands, stapler, binder clips, folders, notepad, paper, clipboard)
- [ ] Snacks like fruit, nuts, energy bars, or other foods that won't melt, create a mess, or drain your energy
- [ ] E-mail sign-up sheet or guest book
- [ ] Mints, toothpicks, or floss
- [ ] Roll of toilet paper (for outdoor shows for when the port-a-johns run out)
- [ ] Paper towels/rags
- [ ] Hand sanitizer
- [ ] Hat
- [ ] Bug spray and sunscreen for outdoor warm-weather events
- [ ] Hand warmers for outdoor chilly-weather events
- [ ] Lip balm
- [ ] First-aid kit (aspirin, Band-Aids, antacid, etc.)
- [ ] Apron (with pockets), tool belt, or fanny pack to stash everything you need to carry around with you
- [ ] Duct tape and twine
- [ ] Plastic sheeting (in case of rain)

You might also consider bringing along an extra pair of shoes and extra socks. After a long day of standing around, you'll find that changing into flip-flops from heavy sneakers or even into a dry pair of socks can be a great refresher.

Top: This indoor display shows off the range of products nicely. Using a simple black background highlights the colors of all the products. **Bottom:** A pegboard can be versatile for a show, allowing you to easily rearrange your products and display effortlessly.

Top: A simple white backdrop and risers can make all the difference in highlighting small pieces. **Bottom:** This craft booth takes advantage of the vertical space, making shoppers feel like they're in a retail setting.

A sign on the exterior of your booth is necessary. Make sure it is consistent with your brand and products.

Top: Space is often much tighter at an indoor craft fair. You may need to find ways to display your wares more creatively. **Bottom:** Demonstrating your craft can attract curious buyers as well as help them understand the effort that goes into making a product.

Group crafting encourages people to exercise their creativity and gets them excited about handmade things. Organizing a make-and-take area at a craft fair or throwing a craft event helps build interest in your work and the craft community.

Top: Providing promotional materials to your speakers and other fans prior to a conference or fair can be helpful to any crafty event. **Bottom:** Branded swag bags are just one way you can get sponsors to participate in your event and makes a nice thank-you for attendees.

Chapter

7

TALKING
SHOP

- -

If you're looking for another outlet for your crafty wares, selling your goods in a brick-and-mortar retail shop is an option you'll want to explore. Selling in shops that work on a consignment or wholesale basis can offer you many advantages, but there are also a number of questions you should ask yourself before starting down this path.

While some crafters dive right into selling in physical shops, we recommend that you get your feet wet selling online and at craft fairs first. Before you begin to collaborate with another business, you need to get used to the ebb and flow of production and to develop your budgeting skills. When you are ready, take it one store at a time and gradually work your way up to stocking multiple stores. It may be a while before your production process is large and efficient enough to enable you to contract with many stores—which is not to say you won't get there. Shauna Alterio and Stephen Loidolt of Something's Hiding in Here sell their goods at thirty-five stores—and Sara Selepouchin of Girls Can Tell now contracts with upwards of sixty independent boutiques!

The Upsides

There is a certain thrill that comes from walking through a boutique and seeing items you made from scratch sitting pretty on a shelf. And there's an even bigger thrill that comes from watching customers pick up your items, check them out, try them on, or just smile as they admire them. But the all-out joy comes from getting an e-mail or call from a shop owner saying your inventory has sold out and they need more product from you.

Besides the inward satisfaction that selling at a boutique can provide—not to mention the "cool factor" of being able to tell people where they can buy your goods in real life—there are also some great promotional and monetary benefits that come with the territory.

Reaching New Audiences

Successful sellers who have been in the craft business for many years know that gaining new customers takes time and effort. Whether you're using online advertising, running print ads, or traveling to craft shows in different markets, attracting new customers isn't snap-of-the-fingers easy. But selling in an actual store puts your craft directly in front of an audience who might not be shopping on sites like Etsy or have any desire to spend a day at a craft fair.

Testing Out New Markets

One great way to test different markets is to get your goods into a store and stay in touch with the owner. Shop owners will usually not pick up a product line if they don't think it will sell. Once you start selling with them, typically on a trial basis, they'll see which products sell like hotcakes and which don't move at all. Most shop owners will work with you to figure out how and what to sell at their stores. "They might see a need that their customers are looking for, and they know that we might be able to problem-solve that," says Shauna Alterio of Something's Hiding in Here. Since you and the shop owner are both invested in the bottom line, working closely with an owner can help you determine the goods that are the best fit for that particular market. Knowing how your different products sell can also be a great help when formulating your inventory list for craft shows and figuring out how to market your goods in various cities.

Gaining Fans

Selling in brick-and-mortar shops means you are now part of a close-knit club that works in harmony to promote itself as well as its individual components. What you gain from being part of this club is association with a desirable brand, especially if you've selected your store correctly, as well as a connection and networking outlet with like-minded shoppers and sellers who understand what you do. This new network of shoppers and sellers will add more people to your customer base and can help you navigate more business opportunities that would be a good fit for your wares.

Some (Potential) Downsides

While selling in retail shops can seem exciting, there are also some downsides. Finding the right fit can take a lot of research. Do take the time to thoroughly research any shop you're interested in, including finding out what sells best, who the customers are, what other sellers are saying about the shop, and so on. If you don't put time into this research, you'll be wasting it by applying and making goods that won't sell.

Getting Rejected

Just because you love the cute boutique down the street (and discuss neighborhood happenings with the owner every time you pop in) does not guarantee that the boutique will accept your goods. Plenty of store owners have had to reject friends and neighborhood fans from selling in their shops, because they are looking at their bottom line. A store owner will have a sense of what sells and what doesn't, and if your goods are rejected, it's not about you. You should not take it personally if the shop owner says no. Still, you do need to have a thick skin to deal with rejection, especially if it comes from your favorite store.

Covering Your Overhead

Most independent stores and boutiques that operate on a consignment basis cannot guarantee any sales for their sellers. Getting accepted to sell on consignment does not mean that you will be receiving a paycheck in the near future—or even that you'll ever receive a paycheck at all. You must think about how to cover your overhead and how to set your prices to cover consignment splits.

For example, say you've been selling your screen-printed T-shirts online. Your total overhead cost is $7 per shirt, which covers the cost to buy each shirt, create the print, and sell it online. Online, you sell your shirts for $20 apiece, which means your net profit is $13 per shirt. If you sell a hundred of them per month, your total monthly profit is $1,300.

But this math won't work if you're selling to a shop that works on a consignment basis. If an independent boutique wants a hundred of your shirts to sell on a one-month trial basis with a fifty-fifty consignment split, you must now put up the money for all one hundred shirts ($700). If you still charge only $20 per shirt, the fifty-fifty split will net you a profit of only $3 per shirt, which means that even if all your shirts sell within the month, you'll only make $300 in profit. If you do the multiplication, you'll see that you need to price your shirts at $40 apiece to net what you would have made by selling online.

Should you sell at one price online and another, higher price in the store? Maybe, but you'll need to be ready for pushback from customers asking why they paid more for your shirt at the store, when they could have just gone online and bought it at a much cheaper price. Or you might decide to raise the price of your shirts across the board, so all your customers pay the same for your shirts no matter where they buy them. But this could very well affect your online sales. (For more on setting prices—both retail and wholesale—see the section "Pricing Your Work," page 40.)

In other words, you need to be thinking continually about overhead and about how raising or lowering prices may affect your income. In addition, take into account that some products may turn into a loss if they don't sell on consignment. All crafters need to figure out their overhead in order to calculate the potential for profit and loss.

Meeting Deadlines

If you're not a deadline-oriented person, selling in stores might not be the best fit for you. Store owners need to regularly replenish their shelves so they can make money and keep their business going. Getting accepted to sell in any store is a privilege that should not be taken lightly. If a shop owner tells you that he or she needs your goods to be delivered by the third of every month, you need to make it happen. It's a major annoyance for store owners when they extend a selling opportunity to a crafter and then the crafter is late in delivery and makes excuses regarding why the goods haven't arrived on time. And for the tardy crafter, it's the perfect recipe for not getting asked back.

Planning for Uneven Cash Flow

The retail crafts business is seasonal, with the high sales periods happening around the December holidays and before Valentine's Day, Mother's Day, and Father's Day. The very low sales periods are January and August—just after Christmas and then again when it's too hot for people to want to leave their air-conditioning. You need to find out what a retail store's flow is like during both the high and the low times. Ask the owner what sales are like throughout the year. This information can help you plan and budget wisely and might even affect your decision whether to sell there.

Finding the Shop That's Right for You

As we've mentioned, just because you love to shop at your neighborhood boutique and are friends with the owner does not mean your wares will sell there. You need to take a look at the shop's current inventory, check out the demographic of the customer base, and read online reviews.

What are the economics of the store's neighborhood or town? How much disposable income do people in the area have? Stores in lower-income areas might sell more functional products—"needs"—as opposed to items that can only be considered "wants."

What is the natural environment like? If a store is located in Miami or Arizona, winter clothing items such as scarves and knitted gloves probably won't sell. Customers in specific environments are more likely to buy items that reflect their living situation and lifestyle. Think about customers who are outdoorsy (Denver), urban (New York City), or environmentally conscious (San Diego). Knowing how the natural environment impacts a market can help you pick stores that are right for your products.

What Do the Current Sellers Say?

Another good way of finding out whether a shop is right for you is to talk to other crafters who sell similar goods at that store. You can get a feel for the high and low selling seasons at the shop, and, most important, learn about others' interaction with the shop owner.

Current sellers can give you important feedback about how knowledgeable and organized a shop owner is. This is important, since the shop owner is the one who will be paying you. Other sellers can let you know if checks tend to be late or contain errors, if items go missing or are frequently stolen, or if an owner doesn't understand his or her own market. Since many independent stores enter into three- to four-month contracts with sellers, you need to try to find out up front whether you can work with a specific shop owner before you jump in for an extended period of time.

What Is the Submissions Process?

It's more and more common these days for independent shops to have an online submission process for potential sellers. You need to follow instructions to a tee in order to be considered. It's not only your craftwork that's being judged but also how well you follow instructions and how professionally you present yourself.

Never, ever, *ever* show up to a store unannounced with your wares. This not only looks unprofessional to any shoppers in the store but is also a pet peeve of many store owners. If there are instructions on how to apply online, follow them. If no information exists online, call the shop and ask about the submissions process. Note how long the store says it will take to get back to you. If it's a month, don't call or e-mail the shop two weeks after submitting to ask for a yes-or-no answer. Respect the rules of the application process.

Remember, if a shop says no, this may be no reflection on the quality of your wares. Reasons for rejection can include limited space or seasonal interest. After an initial rejection, you can certainly ask the owner to keep your application on file or to contact you when the time is right. But remember, too, that being a pest will not win you any points.

Consignment or Wholesale?

Most boutique indie shops that sell handmade goods operate on consignment, while larger chain stores buy stock wholesale. (A few indie stores do buy wholesale, as well.) You need to understand both kinds of arrangements to decide which is best for you.

With consignment, you split profits with the store. Terms vary. The split might be fifty-fifty, or it might be sixty-forty—or even seventy-thirty—in the store's favor. Consignment allows you to sell smaller runs of an item, but you have a large amount of overhead to consider.

Wholesale buyers, by contrast, usually order quantities in the hundreds, which they purchase from you directly via invoice. The only overhead to consider is the up-front cost for materials and labor. You should also take note how soon you'll be paid after shipping your wholesale order. This information should be outlined in the terms of your agreement.

If you can produce your items in mass quantities, there is no reason why you shouldn't explore wholesale and try to get your goods into stores that offer such opportunities. But if you are just dipping your toes into the brick-and-mortar world, starting with a smaller store and operating on consignment is probably your best bet.

Either way, you should build your relationship with your clients, whether they're wholesale buyers or shop owners. They can help you perfect your product line and produce sellable items even as you maintain full control of artistic quality and production quantity. Shauna Alterio of Something's Hiding in Here reports: "We've found that the relationship with all these stores is great because they give this direct feedback. They might be like, 'Everybody really likes the blue version, so we're only going to get blue,' or 'People would really rather have three color options versus one.' So developing meaningful relationships with those shops helps us develop our line as well."

Making a Profit

When you start selling in a shop or two via consignment, you need to set budget goals for yourself. For some crafters, selling in a brick-and-mortar shop is more about getting their name out there, promoting their craft business, and using the store as a way to bring more business to their online shop. For others, it's all about the bottom line. As we stated earlier, knowing what your overhead is and how items should be priced will help you gauge your profitability.

Another thing to consider is that not everything you consign will sell. If you give a store fifty pairs of earrings, and twenty-five pairs are returned to you, will you make a profit, break even, or take a loss? What may seem like a loss might actually be a profit when you consider that customers who bought a pair of your earrings from the store may check out your online shop and make further purchases directly from you.

Something like that happened to Ryan and Lucy Berkley, but on a wholesale order. The Berkleys had licensed three of their animal illustrations to Urban Outfitters but found that some people chose to buy directly from them instead. Lucy explains, "I think with Urban Outfitters, a lot of people that are like us find stuff there but then go look for the artist elsewhere. So many Etsy customers said, 'I saw your work at Urban Outfitters, but I wanted to get it from you.' We also just had a lot more to offer as far as options from our website."

Sometimes, what seemed like a good fit between your goods and a certain shop turns out not to be. If you're not making a profit, you need to reevaluate your relationship with the shop. A savvy store owner should be able to tell you whether it's worth trying to sell other products in his or her store or whether it's time to end the relationship and cut your losses. In any case, you need to shake off disappointing sales and figure out your next move, which might involve adjusting your product line or prices, reevaluating your market, or changing your sales strategy. Again, do not take it personally if your items don't move off the shelves. There is a market out there somewhere for your goods; you just need to figure out where it is.

Pop-Up Shops

The pop-up shop phenomenon has been taking off all over the country. Local governments often fund these temporary stores, or they are bankrolled by enterprising space owners who lease their empty storefronts to retailers or artists for brief periods of time—usually only a month or two. Although pop-up shops don't last long, they can improve retail business in a given area, promote the works of local artists and crafters, and give everyone involved practice in running an independent business and creating ties to the local community.

Pop-up shops that sell handmade goods have been a huge hit. Shops such as the Indie Craft Experience Pop-Up Shop in Atlanta, the Temporium in Washington, DC, and Crafty Wonderland Pop-Up Shop in Portland, Oregon, are examples of temporary shops that highlight what handmade retail has to offer.

Torie Nguyen and Cathy Pitters of Portland took the organizing know-how they gained from running the popular Crafty Wonderland fair and opened a pop-up shop in their downtown district in 2010. At the Crafty Wonderland Pop-Up Shop, they stuffed all the fun and excitement of their twice-a-year craft show into a cute brick-and-mortar shop. Supported by the Portland Business Alliance, the store was amazingly successful, and it reopened as a permanent retail shop the following year.

Funding for pop-up shops varies from city to city. If you are interested in starting a pop-up shop or selling at one, you should check with your local government's arts council or your local business association to see what funding opportunities might be available. If you understand how to maneuver through government bureaucracy, have some experience working with other businesses, and can market and promote the venture, you stand a good chance of success.

Some handmade pop-up shops invite specific crafters to participate, while others have an application process. Because many of these shops are grant funded, the time between the start of the planning process and selecting participating artists is usually very short—think in terms of weeks, not months. But if the chance to apply to sell at a particular pop-up shop comes and goes before you even hear about it, don't fret. As these temporary retail projects gain in popularity, they will gain in funding, and there will be more and more opportunities for pop-up shops in cities across the United States.

Owning Your Own Store

If you've sold in a brick-and-mortar shop owned by somebody else, the next logical step might be to own your own retail store. But this is a huge step, and one that should not be taken lightly. As Maggie White of Young Blood Gallery & Boutique in Atlanta wrote on the *Hello Craft* blog, "Do your homework and know what you're getting into if you want to be profitable. Learn the business side ahead of time. We had to learn from our mistakes and there were a lot of them!" Here are some of the things you need to do before opening the shop and once your business is up and running:

The Business Plan

Having a workable business plan is an essential first step. As Philadelphia-based Erin Waxman, of Art Star Gallery & Boutique, wrote on the *Hello Craft* blog: "Take at least a year to research and develop a business plan. Make sure it is something you really want to do because it is a ton of work! It basically becomes your life. Think of everything you would need to spend money on and price it out. We priced out everything from the rent to the paper clips." Be realistic in your research and planning: Is there a market to support your store? How might the economy affect your sales?

Location, Location, Location

Being in the right location can make or break you. Erin Waxman says of finding the right space, "If you don't plan on selling online, you will need to rely heavily on foot traffic." Think of areas where flows of people naturally occur, like a downtown location or one near other popular retail stores. Dave Sakowski, co-owner of Magpie, in Somerville, Massachusetts, wrote on the *Hello Craft* blog: "Do research on the area you want to open the shop in. We made the mistake of opening in a neighborhood that had the wrong demographic for us, and we moved after six months to our current neighborhood, which has been great."

Your Store's Focus

Is your store going to sell gifts? Accessories for the home? Clothing for kids? For adults? What about craft supplies? What handmade items is your neighborhood lacking? If there seems to be a niche to fill, explore the feasibility of focusing on it.

Don't plan on selling every little thing that you like. That can make for a confusing and discombobulated store. You want your customers to know what type of merchandise they can expect to find in your store.

Reevaluating Retail

Even when your shop is a success, you may find that retail selling isn't what you—an artist—want to spend most of your time doing. San Francisco–based artist and illustrator Lisa Congdon provides a case in point. Lisa had a show at Rare Device in New York City in 2007, and during her visit she hit it off with owner Rena Tom. When Rena and her husband moved to San Francisco not long after, Rena asked Lisa to be her business partner in opening a Rare Device store there. About six months later, they launched their small retail/gallery space filled with handmade and artisan goods.

Says Lisa: "Partnering with Rena at Rare Device was something I embarked on as an experiment. I had never worked in retail or owned a retail shop. But the idea of selling was not new. I had sold my own work, but never other people's work. It was real exciting to me, and I wanted to give it a try.

"It was an awesome way to supplement my illustration income. Because I partnered with Rena, who had a lot of experience, I learned so much about retail. I really enjoyed it and had a fantastic time. Over the course of the three and a half years that I co-owned the business, I got busier with other things, mostly my illustration work. I started to question whether I needed this additional revenue stream and whether owning a retail store was a life goal.

"In reality, my life goal was to become an amazing artist and to keep making art. In the end, I had too much on my plate and I needed to let something go. So Rena and I decided to sell the business. Letting the store go freed up a lot of time to pursue goals more near and dear to my heart, and that's exactly what I was looking for."

Serving Your Artists and Your Customers

Be prompt about paying your artists, and work with them to figure out the best products for your store. Erin Waxman says: "If you are selling items on a consignment basis, make sure paying your artists is a priority. Their commission is not your money to spend." You don't want to become the cranky owner who doesn't pay on time and nobody likes. You'll quickly see your profits tank and product become scarce.

Give good customer service. Be polite and friendly, and don't forget to smile. Be an educator about your store and the crafters whose work you stock. Know their stories and how items are made, and you'll be closing sales left and right.

Investing in Your Community

Olivera Bratich of Wholly Craft, in Columbus, Ohio, wrote on the *Hello Craft* blog: "Invest in your community. You're doing this to see independent crafters succeed, so find out what your crafters need to make that happen. Their success is your success." And Kristen Rask, owner of Schmancy Toys, in Seattle, advises on the *Hello Craft* blog: "Talk to other owners and build a community." As she says, running a shop is "a hard thing to do, and you will greatly appreciate the support and advice from people who have been doing this for a while."

Joining a Craft Mafia

Being part of a craft collective or street team can be a great boon to you and your crafty business. Besides getting you out of the house and interacting with people face-to-face, craft collectives can offer opportunities to:

- Network with people who can be potential resources or customers
- Share skills and learn from fellow members
- Gain access to discounts or exclusive offers from other members
- Pool money for larger ad buys in magazines or on websites

Chapter

8

MARKETING

- -

Marketing is an integral part of selling handmade goods. The more your brand is exposed to the world in a positive way, the more your sales will increase. When it comes to marketing, always keep your brand in mind, and think about what it is that makes your product line loved by your customers. Folks who are similar to the people who already love your brand are the audience you will be targeting in your marketing efforts.

At the end of the day, the best marketing is through word of mouth. When you're thinking about going to a new restaurant or you're trying to find a new hair stylist, you probably ask friends their opinion or turn to an online review site like Yelp. Buyers of crafts do the same thing: opinions of people they trust often persuade them to try out a new seller and make that first purchase.

So much of what is purchased online comes from this trusted recommendation engine. When it comes to buying online, San Francisco–based Willo O'Brien, whose WilloToons business coaches creative small-business owners, says, "People are discovering new stuff because somebody in their network posted it somewhere. The more you're leveraging that and providing the opportunity for people to share your content, the more exposure you'll receive."

This recommendation engine also applies to face-to-face interactions. For example, when your customers have a pleasant experience meeting you in person at a craft fair, they will spread the word to their friends. It therefore makes sense to arm your customers with some tools to help them do this. At craft shows, have promotional items like business cards, buttons, and postcards on display and ready for the taking. (And if you're mailing out an order, make sure to include a few extra business cards that your customer can hand out.) Have your customers help you do the work.

Getting Free Publicity

One way you can market yourself is to garner free publicity about your business through reviews, feature stories, and interviews. These can appear online in blogs or in print publications such as newspapers and magazines (which also usually have an online presence these days).

Targeting News Outlets

Before you approach any writer or editor, it's good to know something about lead times and submissions policies. A blog that's published on a daily basis might be willing to do a story on you very soon after you've submitted the idea, whereas your local newspaper might have a lead time of a few days to a week, while your local magazine will have a longer lead time—at least a month in advance. National glossy magazines have the longest lead times—at least three months in advance and often longer. That means if you're planning to send a press release about your handmade Christmas ornaments to your local daily newspaper, you should send it before Thanksgiving. If you're thinking of contacting the national magazine Bust about it, then you should send the release at the beginning of fall. Big publications usually have submissions policies, which they publish on their websites; make sure you read the policies before submitting an idea.

Writing a Good Press Release

When crafting your press release, keep the following in mind:

Keep it precise and to the point. A good press release shouldn't be more than one page. An even better press release gives readers everything they need to know in the first paragraph. To accomplish this, remember the "five Ws and the H": who, what, when, where, why, and how.

Give it a meaningful headline. The headline does not have to be witty, and it shouldn't be too long. It's a quick way for the writer or reporter receiving the release to understand just what the story's about, so cut to the chase. Use active verbs such as *created*, *illustrated*, and *fashioned*, for example.

Provide contact information. Make sure your contact information appears prominently and clearly. A good place to include it is at the very top of the release, under a heading that says, "For more information, contact." If a writer or editor decides to cover your story, it will be easy to get in touch with you for an interview or to request photos or additional information.

Focus on the newsworthy aspect of your story. What exactly are you trying to relay? Has your new accessory line been picked up by a local boutique? Did a celebrity ask you to create a custom order? Whatever your news, make sure that you present it clearly, emphasizing its timeliness.

Include mention of previous press coverage. If you've been featured before in a newspaper or magazine, be sure to refer to it in your press release. You can even take a sentence or two from your previous press—also known as a blurb—and include it in your text. This lets the writer or editor know that others have found your work worth covering, and it increases your chances of being covered again.

Address it to the right person. You don't want to send your press release to everyone, as that is a waste of time. Research who the appropriate editor is, and send it to him or her. An editor whose beat is sports will have no interest in your product line, but the lifestyle editor may. Editors and their "beats" are often listed on a publication's website, along with their contact information. If not, pick up the phone and ask whom you should send your product information to.

A press release is exactly what it sounds like: a written announcement relaying news. The sidebar on page 129 gives you some pointers on writing a good one.

Before you spend time writing a press release, however, ask yourself *why* you want to send one to news outlets. What makes what you have to share news-worthy? Also ask yourself whether your story really suits the news outlets you're intending to target. A high-end luxury magazine that covers the fancy spas in your city will probably not be interested in your homemade body scrubs, but your local newspaper might use your press release as the basis for a story on cheaper alternatives to those expensive spas!

Pitching to Websites and Blogs

Formal press releases are standard in the world of traditional media like newspapers and magazines. If you are reaching out to a blog or website, you can take a less formal approach. That means you can dispense with the headline and adopt an informal tone. If you have already written a press release, do feel free to reuse portions of it when pitching to blogs. Many of the tips for writing press releases—especially keeping your communica-tion short and precise—also apply to

pitching to online outlets. Here are a few more tips:

FIND OUT THE BLOGGER'S NAME—AND USE IT. Hate getting spam? So do bloggers. If you address your e-mail to "Dear Blogger," it just shows you're too careless to bother finding out whom you're contacting. You probably took the time to research the writer's e-mail, and chances are his or her name is right there in the e-mail. Make sure to use it to personalize your pitch. If the blog you are pitching has more than one writer, do a little research to see who would be most likely to cover your work, and send your e-mail to that particular blogger.

DON'T ATTACH TOO MANY PHOTOS—OR ANY HIGH-RESOLUTION PHOTOS. If you feel you must include images to get your point across, include one or, at the most, two low-resolution (small-file-size) photos. Just make sure to note you have high-res photos available, and include a link to them if they're posted online.

KEEP IT SHORT. Make your case why this blog should feature you in one or two paragraphs. If you don't, chances are the blogger will just stop reading. Bloggers receive a ton of e-mail pitches daily, so grab their attention quickly and concisely.

DO YOUR HOMEWORK. Read the blog before you pitch. Why should this blog write about you? Do you make accessories from repurposed clothing that would fit well with the "eco-friendly picks" featured on the blog every Friday? Whatever the reason you think your product will be of interest to the blog's readers, make sure you mention it right off the bat in your e-mail.

CHECK YOUR SPELLING AND LINKS. Not only should you make sure everything is spelled correctly, you should double-check any hyperlink to see that it actually clicks through to the correct website.

IF NECESSARY, UPDATE YOUR ONLINE PRESENCE. Are you linking to your Etsy shop or blog in the e-mail pitch? If so, make sure it's up-to-date.

Buying Advertising

The flip side of free publicity is advertising you have to pay for. The traditional advertising route—purchasing print ads—is on the way out. Buying ads on websites and blogs that will appeal to your target audience is now the way to go.

Before you commit to any online advertising, take time to research the websites you are interested in. Make sure their editorial content is something your customers (present and future) are likely to be interested in. If you have no idea where to start looking, click around on the websites and blogs you already read, then check their blog rolls. If you are really stuck, ask crafters and customers you correspond with what their favorite sites are.

Before buying an online ad, gather information about various sites' metrics, the

A Good Blog Pitch

A good pitch is short, sweet, and personable and provides all the pertinent information you are trying to convey. Here's a great example:

> Hi, Kelly!
>
> I'm a big fan of Hello Craft and have been greatly enjoying the "Craft Idol" column posted every Friday. I think I have a crush on Jon Wye. Shhh!
>
> I've been working very hard on my latest fabric line and would be honored if you would consider me for a "Craft Idol" post. My fabric line is perfect for crafters looking for fun and edgy prints that are also eco-friendly!
>
> My favorite is the rotten apple print.
>
> Attached is a full press release announcing my new line. You can view all the fabrics on my website, at superawesomefabricsmadebyme.com
>
> Thanks so much for looking.
>
> Happy crafting!
> Lauren
>
> Super Awesome Fabrics Made by Me
> 123 Awesome Street
> Awesometown, USA
> Lauren@superawesomefabricsmadebyme.com
> 555-555-5555

This pitch is personable, timely, and shows that "Lauren" knows her audience and is a reader of the blog. She references actual posts on the blog and asks to be included in a specific column. She includes all her contact information, attaches a full press release, and gives the blogger a way to view all of the products in her line.

demographic profiles of their audiences, and the geographical locations of their visitors. This will help you decide which sites will serve you best. Some sites may have a page with this information, or they will e-mail you the stats on request. You can also conduct research through market analysis sites like Alexa (alexa.com), Compete (compete.com), and Quantcast (quantcast.com). You can get basic information such as traffic numbers and rankings for free. More in-depth analysis costs money.

When you start contacting websites and blogs, compare their prices before you commit to anything. Factor in the duration your ad will have on the site. Also find out where your online ad will appear. Will it be placed close to editorial content? Will you see it onscreen when you first load the page—that is, will it be "above the fold"—or will you have to scroll down to see it? Find out, too, whether it's possible to work out a deal that involves cross-promotion or partnerships, such as a giveaway on the website. And will the website provide you with stats after the advertisement has completed its run online?

When you have narrowed down your choices, make sure there is a clear plan that both parties agree to fulfill, including the length of time the advertisement will run and at what cost.

You'll also need to find out the design specifications—the "specs"—for the ad you'll be submitting. If you're not a skilled, web-savvy graphic designer, you may have to hire someone to design the ad for you. Specs include the following:

- The dimensions of the advertisement (usually expressed in pixels)
- The maximum file size
- Whether static, animated, or flash files are accepted, and the preferred file format (.gif, .tiff, .pdf, .png, or .swf)

After you have done the research and bought web advertisements, keep an eye on your analytics. Be sure the click-through URL you provide to the websites you're advertising on is one you can track through your own analytics. That way, you can figure out which ads are bringing more traffic to your own site.

Doing Your Own Marketing

Before taking on your own marketing campaign, identify how much time you have available to spend on it. Make a log of how many hours you dedicate each week to each aspect of your business—designing your product line, producing it, and selling it. Then see whether you can fit in a block of time each day to devote to marketing efforts.

Besides garnering free press coverage and buying advertising, you can also spend time engaging your current and potential customer base via various social media, including Facebook, Flavors.me, Flickr, Foursquare, LinkedIn, Pinterest, Twitter, and Tumblr. Each social media platform has its own pros and cons and set of rules and standards. Research which ones make sense to you and your business by finding out where your audience is. And remember that social media move at the speed of lightning, so what you use today may not be around tomorrow. Be flexible and learn to adapt. (For more on using social media, see page 138.)

Another avenue to explore is sending out e-mail newsletters to your customers, fans, and wider community. You can gather an e-mail list by having a sign-up right on your website and by collecting addresses during craft fairs. It is important to make sure your e-mail list is opt-in, meaning each person makes a decision to receive your e-mails. Make it clear to people what they are signing up for, and don't share your list without their consent or add your customers' e-mail addresses to your newsletter list without their say-so. No one likes being spammed with unwelcome correspondence! (Plus, it's illegal.) Try to space out your newsletters so that each one has *new* stories and interesting tidbits to share. At Hello Craft, we send out our newsletters on a regular basis unless there's really exciting news to share that warrants a stand-alone e-mail, such as announcing the Summit of Awesome. The following are some programs that can help you manage your e-mail list:

AWeber (aweber.com)
Constant Contact (constantcontact.com)
iContact (icontact.com)
MailChimp (mailchimp.com)
VerticalResponse (verticalresponse.com)
YMLP (yourmailinglistprovider.com)

You Don't Have to Do It All Yourself

An Interview with Jena Coray

Jena Coray of the Miss Modish publicity agency, based in Portland, Oregon, offers marketing and PR services to artists and makers interested in taking their business to the next level. We asked her about the kinds of things a publicist can accomplish and about her approach to helping crafters achieve their business goals.

Q: **When is it time for an independent business owner to consider paying someone to work on marketing and PR?**

A: If I could tell my just-starting-in-business self one thing I think it'd be: *You don't have to do it all yourself!* There is just not enough time (or inclination) in a day to become an expert at all the vital skills you'll need to create a healthy, thriving business. So I think, from the outset, it's important to consider which aspects of marketing, branding, and PR best align with your natural skills. Focus on those so you can make the most effective, fun, and profitable use of your time, and plan on hiring professionals to help you with the rest.

In terms of marketing efforts, that could mean hiring a skilled graphic designer to create your logo, website, or branding. Or a copywriter to help with product descriptions or an engaging "about" page. A photographer to shoot your product photographs or a lookbook. A PR rep to help gain media exposure for your brand. Or a consultant to create a marketing plan and offer branding, blogging, or social media advice.

I think it's essential to invest in your business by working with professionals on things where your particular skill set is lacking. And remember, that doesn't always mean paying out the ear. There are indie-budget-friendly helpers in every sector of marketing, coaching, and branding. Talented friends who work for cookies and fellow indie business owners that like to trade skill for skill. Let other talented people help with the stuff you're not so good at, so you can spend your time getting *even better* at what you're *best* at.

Q: **What are some marketing tasks that people can do themselves and manage day to day on their own?**

A: Marketing is in every communication you have with your customers and potential customers, whether you're speaking directly to them or your website is doing the talking for you. You want that association to be one of trust, respect, and excitement to see what's next from you.

That means providing really excellent customer service, every gosh darn day. Engaging and conversing with "your people" authentically, both through social media and real life. It means blogging in an open way that shares true pieces of yourself to help form personal connections with your readers. It means commenting on other blogs, being a fan of folks, supporting fellow indies that you admire and people in the same field as you. Conversation *is* marketing. What do you want the conversations about your brand to be?

Q: It's subjective for each individual, but, generally speaking, what is the right mix of paid advertising versus free press for someone's first marketing and PR campaign?

A: Generally speaking, I think it's good to have a mix of paid-for advertising/sponsorship features along with a continual effort to pitch yourself to appropriate blogs/editorials. Advertising on targeted blogs that speak to the audience you're hoping to reach can be a great way to establish a consistent presence for your brand. That consistency helps build recognizability, reliability, and trust in your brand with your potential customers. It's especially essential when just starting out, I think, to gain visibility for a new business. Goals for your advertising efforts should not be all about direct sales. Advertising can help you assess which types of markets align with your brand the best so you can focus on those, while helping you gain exposure to new audiences and increasing traffic to your site along the way. Advertising is about making people aware of you. Awareness comes first, then trust, then the sale.

Along with advertising and working on building your relationships with customers (as mentioned earlier) you'll also want to start introducing yourself to blogs and editorials. This could mean "pitching" your shop to blogs that serve your niche and feature products often. Or if you're in a service business, you can seek out guest blogging opportunities as a way to introduce your skills to a new audience and reaffirm your skills to those who already know of you. Or, as any kind of designer, maker, or creative person, you probably have a good eye, a cool workspace, and some stories to tell, so seek out interviews, submit photos of your studio/house to blogs that do tours, and submit project tutorials and freebies you create to blogs that feature them. And say yes to participating in projects that seem like they'll utilize your talents in new, fun ways while increasing exposure for your brand at the same time. Because engaging, effective marketing starts with doing what feels right, fun, and true to you.

Q: **What are some goals and benchmarks for people to keep in mind when making their first big marketing push?**

A: Everyone's goals are going to be different, really, depending on the nature of their business and where they're at with it, but it is helpful to set objectives at the beginning of any marketing or PR "push." You'll want to set *specific* goals that you'd like to achieve over a *defined period of time.*

For example, one of your goals could be to get at least three editorial mentions on great blogs over the next month. Or to increase your website traffic average from 50 visitors per day to 150 over the next month. Set your goals and then work backward to set milestones for yourself to achieve them.

If you're aiming for three blog mentions in one month, maybe you should start by pitching to three or four blogs each week—schedule it in, do it, see how long it takes to get your first write-up. If you'd like to triple your web traffic over a month, try placing an ad on two or three different targeted sites at a time (as budget allows) to see which one gives you the best ratio of traffic for your money. Or try blogging like crazy one month and see if that affects your traffic positively. Or get more active on Twitter and Facebook every day for a month and see if that affects your traffic.

Have fun, play, and experiment with different techniques. Review and adjust the methods along the way, as you learn what works best for you, and make those goals happen!

Using New Technology for Marketing

When it comes to new technology, it is definitely important to keep your ear to the ground. Technology moves so fast. Trends that are popular today might be worthless in a few years. A case in point is Friendster. At one point, it was the leading social media site, with 8 million users; now it's just a gaming site with a little more than 1 million members.

It's not necessary to jump on the bandwagon with each new trend as it pops up.

It's much more important to engage and interact with your customer and fan base where they already are. Conduct research to find out the demographics of the users of the particular social media site(s) you may want to use. Are they the same as your customers? If yes, then it makes sense to set up a profile and engage your fans there.

Also, you should have fun. Diane Koss of Cutesy But Not Cutesy has created a large monster mascot that she videos interacting with people in real life. These videos, which appear on YouTube, provide a great example of how new technology can be used to market and extend a brand. Diane says about her videos: "I love bringing the monster out in public and seeing reactions or nonreactions that people have. Do they try to ignore it, or are they scared it's going to do something to them? The idea of the videos is to create a buzz about the monsters." She wants the videos to evolve into a blog for the monster mascot, where people can send pictures or videos of their monster sightings.

One technology that's guaranteed to continue to grow in the near future is the smartphone. Have you tried viewing your own website or online store on a smartphone? If not, put down this book and do it right now. Is it easy to navigate? Does it work on all different kinds of phones? (Test it out on your friends' phones to see.) What about on a tablet? If not, take steps to make your online presence work on the mobile web, or consider hiring someone to improve it for you.

It is important to keep up with trends so you can identify what will work best for your business: QR codes that can be read by mobile phones? Text messaging? Mobile payments? Bookmark websites that report on new trends in technology, and read them regularly to learn what's newly available and how you might use it. Here are a few such sites:

> Advertising Age, especially the site's *DigitalNext* blog (adage.com)
> American Express OPEN Forum (openforum.com)
> Lifehacker (lifehacker.com)
> Mashable (mashable.com)
> The Next Web (thenextweb.com)
> ReadWriteWeb (readwriteweb.com)
> TechCrunch (techcrunch.com)
> VentureBeat (venturebeat.com)

You have to decide for yourself what the right mix of new technologies is for marketing your business. And you've got to keep evaluating what you are using, and change it up if it's not getting your message across. Sue Eggen of Giant Dwarf used to mostly use Flickr to post product photos, but to increase her online presence she decided to use Facebook, too. Sue says, "I believe you have to focus on what's available to the people, and what's available to the people is Twitter and Facebook. I love Flickr. I think it's great, but at the same time I need to swim around Flickr and go towards the popular social networks."

Finally, let us repeat: In all your marketing efforts, it is crucial to keep your brand in mind. If you stay true to yourself, you'll attract customers who love you for the right reason—being uniquely yourself.

Chapter

9

EXPANDING YOUR
BUSINESS

A t a certain point, you'll have to decide whether or not to grow your business and, if so, at what pace. Sometimes growth will happen organically, where opportunities easily come your way, and you find yourself excitedly saying yes to them all. But at other times, you'll need to guide your business in the direction that will help you get to the next level. And sometimes exponential growth comes overnight, so the more you can do to prepare for it now, the better able you'll be to take advantage of the opportunity when it arises.

This amorphous "next step" will be different for everyone, depending on your ultimate goal. It might mean hiring workers to increase your production, going to trade shows, and pursuing wholesale buyers. If so, it's necessary to figure out everything you'll need to fulfill wholesale orders. There are so many issues to consider. As Dale Dougherty, cofounder of O'Reilly Media and the publisher of *Make* magazine, said in the April 2011 issue of *Inc.* magazine, "Even the most successful crafters run up against the limits of their own labor. Handmade can be a limited idea." But *limited* is a harsh word. As crafters know, it is up to you to define your "limits."

Diversifying Your Income

Expanding your business doesn't necessarily mean scaling up the production of your product line. It can also mean diversifying your income. For many crafters, this is the norm, and they don't think of it as having "multiple revenue streams." But, in fact, that's what you have if you're selling online in three different places as well as selling in person at craft fairs. Basically, anything you do that generates income is a revenue stream. Besides selling at craft fairs and online stores, your revenue streams might include the following:

- Selling via your own website
- Selling ads on your website or blog
- Selling via a gallery
- Self-publishing
- Licensing your work
- Pattern making
- Doing paid speaking gigs
- Teaching workshops or classes

And this list can go on and on.

Many crafters find having multiple income streams to be very rewarding. Being able to focus on different areas of the business each day can help keep you motivated and excited about your work. Says illustrator Lisa Congdon, "I really like having a lot of things going on. It keeps things more interesting for me."

For some indie crafters, writing, self-publishing, and teaching aren't merely supplemental revenue streams but major sources of income. That's true, for example, of Diane Gilleland, who writes the *CraftyPod* blog. And, like other crafters, Diane needs more than one income stream to make a living. As she recalls: "The early books I read on the subject were all about the model of making something and then selling the finished goods. There was just so much talk in those books about how challenging it is to make a good income and all these strategies because you have production time and marketing time. You had to do every aspect of it. So I got all of that absorbed in my brain as this message of, 'I'm going to have to figure out how to do more than one thing because it's really hard to make enough of a living from doing one thing in craft.'" So Diane did podcasts for a publisher and some freelance craft writing, then moved on to do craft project designs and self-published e-books and, later, to teach online classes.

One problem with having so many income streams is that you really need to stay on top of everything to make it work. With all the upkeep each revenue stream requires, your attention will be divided, so make sure you keep track of all your responsibilities and deadlines and of where the money will be coming from and when it will be coming in and going out.

Lee Meredith of leethal.net recommends being open "to weird opportunities" but also to think extra hard about taking nonpaying jobs, as they are "iffy." She says, "Sometimes they can lead to good work, so don't say no without thinking about it, as it might be a good idea to do it." If you are not going to be paid for your work, what else will you be getting out of the experience? Maybe there are invaluable connections to be made, or maybe the exposure is worth more than a paycheck. Things that don't pay now can have a way of paying off in the future, though this may not be readily apparent.

When deciding what to do next, Diane Gilleland falls back on a piece of advice she read in Barbara J. Winter's book *Making a Living without a Job* (New York: Bantam, 2009). Winter suggests setting aside one hour each workday for future income planning—she calls it the "one-hundred-dollar hour." Diane explains: "That was where she tested new ideas or just did research on stuff she thought she might make money on. The point was that it was so easy to get caught up in your day-to-day maintenance that you forget that sooner or later as an entrepreneur you're going to have to reinvent yourself again."

Licensing Your Work

As the creator of your work you have the right to license it. This basically means you can enter into a contract with another party and legally give them some or all the rights to produce, distribute, and sell the work. Why might you want to do this? For the simple reason that licensing your work can open up a new market for your designs and brand—one you wouldn't be able to reach on your own.

When licensing your work, you'll need a clear written contract outlining where, when, and how the agreement will be fulfilled; each party's responsibilities; and the length of the contract. It should specify what products or designs are being licensed, where they can be sold geographically, your royalty (that is, the percentage of income you will receive from sales), the advance payment (if any) you will receive, and whether the agreement is exclusive or nonexclusive.

Be aware that there are pros and cons to exclusive licensing agreements. Exclusivity can give you the option of running special editions in limited quantities, and you may get a better overall deal if the contract is exclusive. But you don't want to put yourself in a situation where another opportunity comes along and you have to sit it out because you've already signed away those rights in an exclusive contract.

Ryan and Lucy Berkley have had great experiences with licensing. They took advantage of two opportunities, one with Urban Outfitters and the other with Jenny Hart of Sublime Stitching. They licensed three of Ryan's animal images to Urban Outfitters, which arranged for print runs of 1,000 to 1,500 each; the final product was a framed print, with Ryan's name on a big sticker on the back of each print. The Berkleys earned a royalty of approximately 2 percent from each sale, which is typical for this type of licensing deal. "They gave Ryan credit and a little bio on the website. It was awesome. We found that they paid us in a timely manner. The exposure that it gave us is probably what has sustained our business over the last year and a half," Lucy says of the experience.

Jenny Hart approached the Berkleys about doing an embroidery pattern for her. Both Lucy and Ryan were big fans of Sublime Stitching and already owned many of Jenny's patterns. "It was flattering. We were very excited," Ryan says. Jenny licensed four of their animal images—the rabbit, the cat, the fox, and the robin—translating Ryan's drawings into the embroidery patterns herself. Their licensing deal is indefinite, and Jenny pays the Berkleys quarterly based on how many patterns she sells per quarter. "One of our favorite things is when people are buying the kits and embroidering themselves and posting pictures. We just like to see other people interpret the artwork. It's interesting," Ryan says.

Selling Wholesale

Selling wholesale is a great opportunity and will provide a lot of exposure to you and your brand. To be ready to sell wholesale, you need to have your production down to a science and be able to fulfill large orders.

Showing at Trade Shows

One way to break into wholesale is by exhibiting at trade shows. Trade shows are similar to craft fairs, but they're directed at buyers for retail stores rather than at individual consumers. Just as you would if you were thinking of selling at a craft fair, you'll need to research which trade shows your products are most appropriate for. You'll want to find out about the kinds of buyers who attend a given show and also whether crafters who do work similar to yours show there and, if so, what kind of success they've had.

Trade shows offer amazing opportunities. You get to see what else is out there, and you can interact directly with buyers, who will let you know why your product is good for their market or not. Doing a trade show is also great exposure. Sara Selepouchin of Girls Can Tell started out doing the Buyers Market of American Craft in Philadelphia, where she made a lot of connections. Rhonda and Elijah Wyman of

Figs & Ginger were able to quit their day jobs in 2007, when they started doing the Buyers Market and the American Craft Council shows. Rhonda says, "We had never done anything like that before—it was amazing. We took in over $15,000 worth of orders, and we had never seen that much money in our life."

A downside to consider is that trade shows are quite expensive to exhibit at. Costs include application fees, booth fees, shipping costs, and possibly rental charges for tables, chairs, and other equipment. Sometimes you have to pay for electricity to power additional lamps or your laptop. Such charges are likely to be much higher than those at your local craft fair. Many trade shows are held in large convention centers that contract with unions to set up the show. Be sure to review the rules and regulations on what you can do yourself during setup and what needs to be handled by a union worker. Transport of your merchandize to and from your booth and setup of tables and chairs will probably be under the purview of union labor.

After being in business for almost fifteen years, Queen Bee Creations started doing trade shows in 2009. As owner Rebecca Pearcy explains, she'd resisted doing the shows because the cost was prohibitive. But then, she says, "As the market changed and the economy changed, we shifted gears and became more proactive. Those little boutiques were having a really hard time meeting our minimums or ordering with any regularity because their business had changed so much." So Rebecca took Queen Bee to trade shows to get her work out in front of new people and new shops, and to be more competitive.

Other Wholesale Opportunities

Wholesale orders don't come exclusively through trade shows. There are even crafters who get wholesale orders without ever doing trade shows. For example, the chain store Anthropologie approached Sue Eggen, of Giant Dwarf, wanting to purchase a run of one hundred of her rosette fascinator headpieces. At the time,

Sue was a one-woman operation, or, as she jokingly puts it, "Well, you can count me as an employee, I guess. 'She' helped me night and day with that order, and there was blood, sweat, and tears from both of 'us.' 'We' were determined to get that order out." The work was extremely labor-intensive, since each fascinator had to be cut, sewn, and packaged by hand. "It took me forever," Sue says.

Once Sue completed the order, Anthropologie came back with another one—this time for five hundred pieces. "I had to decline," she laments. "It broke my heart. I said, 'I'm really sorry. There is no way.' I would probably lock myself in a cage somewhere and never ever speak to a human being again. I was done. I didn't want to sell anymore. I was so burnt and unmotivated and uninspired. It really sucked. I didn't want my life to be that way."

Sarah and Victor Lytvinenko, of Raleigh Denim, had a somewhat similar experience when they were approached by a buyer from Barneys New York. Sarah recalls, "That first order was for 114 pairs of jeans. Victor and I sewed every single pair. We didn't have a cutting table or anything." Her father lent a hand, putting in all the rivets with a hand press, and both of their moms helped to iron the seams and package the jeans. "In terms of production and manufacturing, we did everything," Sarah says.

Trade Shows and Sales

Typically, a *trade show* is open only to buyers, whereas a *trade show and sale* is open both to buyers and to the general public. At a trade show, you should expect to sell only at wholesale prices. At a show and sale, you should expect a period of time open only to wholesale buyers followed by a period of time when the event is open to the public—at which point you should change to normal retail pricing.

ACRE. The American Craft Retailers Expo takes place in Las Vegas, Nevada, and showcases traditional fine craft.

American Craft Council. The ACC produces public shows across the country, showcasing traditional fine craft as well as some indie crafts.

Buyers Market of American Craft. The ACC produces this wholesale show in Baltimore; sellers include makers of traditional fine craft as well as some indie crafts.

CHA Conference and Trade Show. The oldest craft and hobby trade show is held in January and June.

National Stationery Show. This trade show has to do with all things paper and takes place in New York.

New York International Gift Fair. The NYIGF offers wholesale opportunities to sellers whose products qualify as "gifts." It takes place in New York City twice a year—in summer and again in winter.

One of a Kind Show and Sale. OOAK specializes in handcrafted items and is open to the indie aesthetic. There are two shows in Canada and one in Chicago.

Pool Tradeshow. Pool is held twice a year (February and August) in Las Vegas. Regarded as ultrahip and modern, it caters specifically to boutique stores.

San Francisco International Gift Fair. The West Coast sister of NYIGF, the SFIGF is a little more design oriented.

SOFA. The International Expositions of Sculpture Objects & Functional Art showcases fine art, design, and decorative art. There are several Sofa shows, though the main show takes place in Chicago.

Surtex. This art and design show, held in New York City, attracts a thousand artists and designers looking to sell and license their work.

Their first order did so well that Barneys came back to them before the season was over. They were not expecting it. That second order was double the first, and then Barneys placed another order that doubled the amount again. Sarah says, "We actually didn't have enough money to buy the materials by the time our second or third order came around. It's a huge cost up front." They were able to accept and fulfill these orders only because they had obtained a loan via the stimulus package that had just been signed into law.

By contrast, Sara Selepouchin of Girls Can Tell—who *had* exhibited at shows—felt prepared when Anthropologie contacted her for a wholesale order. But this order didn't come through a trade show. As Sara recalls, "They e-mailed sort of out of the blue. I had been in *Country Living* magazine, and when they e-mailed me, they said they found me on Etsy; then they mentioned they had found me in *Country Living* as well. I met with my buyer, and she was super-friendly, and I gave her samples to keep in the office. One day, she said, she had put up my towels in the hallway—they gauge how well a product will do on the market by how many people in the office stop to look at a product—and everyone was stopping to look at my work."

Anthropologie ordered several thousand pieces of Sara's screen-printed designs, spread out over a handful of orders. Sara prints, packages, and ships the orders to the chain's distribution center, from which her products are shipped to stores all over the country. About her involvement with wholesale, Sara says, "It forced me to grow up as a company. It's been amazing, and it's helping to take things to the next level."

Wholesale Buyers' Expectations

Buyers for retail stores expect a high level of craftsmanship and professionalism from their wholesale suppliers. This doesn't mean you should be inauthentic to your brand, but that your product line should be fully developed and present a clear and cohesive look. You want the buyers to be able to imagine putting your work in their stores and believing that your work will sell in their stores.

When you do a trade show, have an e-mail list at your booth where buyers can sign up to stay informed of your goings-on. E-mail them your newsletter, which can help keep you in their mind for future sales. Make sure you bring along enough marketing materials—postcards, business cards, and line sheets—for all potential buyers to take away.

A line sheet is a very important tool when selling at a trade show. A line sheet lists all the products you have for wholesale, with an image, a detailed description (including materials and dimensions), and the wholesale price and minimum order for each piece. Your line sheet should look like a natural extension of your brand.

Setting Order Minimums

A minimum order is the base amount of a particular item that a buyer must purchase. You can set order minimums at any level you are comfortable with—starting at just one. And different items can have different minimums. Say your line of products includes a variety of bags, purses, and wallets. You might want to set a minimum of twenty-five for your small cotton coin purses, but a minimum of five for your large leather messenger bags. Remember that if you set your minimum order in the hundreds, you have to be prepared to fulfill that order, plus any additional items a buyer may want to purchase.

Wholesale Pricing

Wholesale pricing is different from retail pricing. After you've calculated what your per-item retail pricing should be, cut that in half to determine your wholesale price. If that seems like too big a hit for your business to sustain, think about whether you were honest with yourself when setting your retail price. You want to be able to make a living, and if you're underselling yourself, you're not only hurting your- self but also devaluing the entire hand- made community. (For more on setting

prices—both retail and wholesale—see the section "Pricing Your Work," page 40.)

Fulfilling Orders

When you sell wholesale, you have to be ready to fulfill your orders, making the products and shipping them out in a timely manner. So be sure you have enough sup- plies, resources, and help ready to go when the order comes in. Be realistic about this. As Shauna Alterio of Something's Hiding in Here says: "Saying that you want to do wholesale is great, but being able to deliver the goods on time is such a big thing to us. We never want to let those people down, because we've seen how fruitful those relationships are. We never want to get ourselves in a situation where we need one more week. It's really time consuming when you are making things by hand. Most people understand that, but not everyone does."

Hiring Help

As you can see, showing at trade shows and accepting wholesale orders can be an ambitious goal. When Sue Eggen of Giant Dwarf got burned out from filling orders, her fiancé told her, "Hire somebody. You need to hire somebody. In order to grow, you need to hire someone." Many successful crafters come to this inevitable conclusion: if they want to sustain and grow a successful business, the next necessary step is to hire some help.

"That's not an easy transition to make," Shauna Alterio says. "To go from making everything yourself to learning how to let other people do it for you. Being able to keep up with that demand while keeping it handmade is a very tricky balance." Not only do you need to learn how to give up control, but hiring an employee opens up a whole new—and sometimes quite complicated—can of worms. Basically, you now have to learn to be your own human resources department. You have to figure out where to look for help, what skills you want in an employee, how to conduct the hiring process, and how to train and manage the employee. In other words, you've got to learn how to be the boss.

Contract Workers Versus Payroll Employees

When you hire someone, will you be contracting the work out or bringing the person onto your business's payroll? There are pros and cons to each arrangement, and what works best for you will depend on where you are in your business and what you can afford. Remember that with payroll, you have to pay payroll taxes for each employee, whereas if you contract out the work, the contractor is responsible for those taxes, and the arrangement may therefore be less expensive for you. But a word of caution here: if you hire contract workers and have them come to your place of business (your office, studio, retail shop), you may be in violation of IRS classification and opening yourself up to fines and back taxes. Research the rules and regulations regarding contract versus payroll employees very carefully to make sure you are in compliance.

Kasey and Kelly Evick of Biggs and Featherbelle feel that payroll employees are preferable to contract workers. Says Kasey, "It costs us more to make them employees, but it's better for them. They will make more money, and it makes them be more serious about us as a company. They are more loyal."

Some crafters pay under the table the people who help them, but this is *not* a good idea. There is no recourse for either employer or employee if something goes wrong. "I can see why people pay under the table because it's so expensive to have employees, but it's best to do it legally," says Rhonda Wyman of Figs & Ginger. "We've had part-time employees, but now we just have an independent contractor. Having an employee is a lot of responsibility and pressure. It's intimidating and stressful."

Rebecca Pearcy of Queen Bee Creations warns, "It is a really, really big step, and it is really intimidating, and it's a lot of responsibility to have employees." When Rebecca realized she had to bring on an employee, she knew she had to get serious: "I just was like, okay, I need to make this official, and on the up-and-up. That's when I started doing the official thing, taking the payroll taxes out and everything. It was terrifying." It is wise to seek the help of an accountant

Contract or Payroll?

Contract Workers	Payroll Employees
Are responsible for paying their own taxes	Have payroll taxes deducted from their paycheck
Receive a 1099 form from each employer reporting all wages paid during the previous year	Are subject to employment laws
May be paid on an hourly, per-piece, or flat-rate basis	May be salaried or paid on a per-hour basis
Are expected to fulfill the contract as agreed	• Can leave your employ at will • Must follow employee rules that you establish • May be more loyal to you and your company

when setting up your system for doing payroll and paying payroll taxes. You want to make sure you are not hurting your employees or your business by making mistakes.

Creating and Managing a Team

Employee protocol—hiring, firing, and maintaining a professional relationship with and between your employees—involves a number of skills that you will have to learn. About her own experience, Queen Bee Creations' Rebecca Pearcy says, "It just took doing it a bunch of times to get better at it, in terms of finding the right people, interviewing, the skills involved in hiring, and then creating an environment that people want to stay in. I find when I ask for feedback from people that work with me that so much of what they enjoy about where they work is the people they work with."

Creating a culture that people want to work in and have an investment in is a tall order. But your vision for your handmade company and the ideals that got you into this lifestyle can translate into a work environment that will attract people who find your ideals appealing. Raleigh Denim's Sarah and Victor Lytvinenko learned that they needed to hire "people that are happy to be here." Sarah says, "In many cases, skill can be taught. If there is a problematic situation, address it as soon as possible. It's really hard to do at times, but it's better to bite the bullet and keep our work atmosphere as upbeat as we can."

You need to set boundaries between your work and your personal life. Of Queen Bee's work environment, Rebecca Pearcy says, "We're pretty clear about how hard we work. You're at work. It's not like a party. We go to happy hour and socialize and get to know each other, but we're definitely pretty serious about what we do."

Some people find it easy to be friends with their employees, but that can become tricky if the economy tanks and you can no longer afford to keep your friends in your employ. Says Rebecca, "I find it easier for me to do my job as an employer if I have a clear boundary between work and personal life, in terms of who I am at work and what I choose to share about my life, and how I choose to have relationships with my employees. I love to have very friendly relationships with my employees, but I definitely have my friends outside of work, and my employees are different."

An Employer's Perspective: Queen Bee Creations

Rebecca Pearcy's Queen Bee Creations has grown from one employee to fifteen people today. That's an increase of about one person for every year Queen Bee has been in business. When Rebecca started to bring on help, it was a natural step.

"It became obvious," she recalls. "I think I was a bit in denial. Redd [her friend and first employee] was like, 'You're going to need some help,' and I was like, 'Really? Okay.' He was the one who clued me in to the fact that I needed somebody. He was right. And that's the thing: sometimes you don't realize it until you've hired somebody, or you start delegating, and you're just like, 'Oh my God, I can't believe I didn't do this sooner. What was I waiting for?'"

She continues, "I've been advised many times to just keep focusing on what is truly my job, which is design, the creative part, and coming up with new ideas and new products and designs, and that if somebody else can do something else, then somebody else should be doing it. If somebody else can do the bookkeeping, let somebody else do the bookkeeping. If somebody else can run production, let somebody else run production, that kind of thing. It literally became, okay, I was doing everything. And then, one by one, I took my hands off as many of those things as I could.

"It's an ongoing process. It's not like I get to spend every hour at work just designing. I'm still trying to get there. No matter what, if you're the owner, the head of a company, and you're also the creative person, there's always going to be the running of the business, unless you have a business partner whose focus that is. You know, you're probably the one who's going to have to go talk to the lender at the bank if you need capital to work with. You're going to have to come up with the vision to guide the company. There are just some things that are not the cutting and sewing and crafting and making that are involved in running the company, for sure."

Craft as Fine Art

Does your craft cross the boundary into the fine-art arena? If so, that may give you some new avenues to pursue, including having your work sold in galleries and maybe even having it shown in museums. This can be a tricky line to walk, however, as some galleries draw a very definite line between what is craft and what is art. But it's also true that there's an ever-expanding gray area between the craft world and the art world.

Selling in Galleries

To sell in galleries, you have to play by a somewhat different set of rules than those that apply to selling in retail craft shops. Galleries are more rigid in the way they

operate, and crafters may find this stifling.

While it may be difficult to break into the art world, the silver lining is that the more shows you do, the easier it will become to get into other shows. To find appropriate galleries that may be interested in showing your work you need to conduct the same kind of research you would regarding any outreach you might do. Start by researching upcoming local shows that look interesting. Are there any "unconventional" spaces—such as coffee shops, bars, restaurants, or non-craft retail shops—in your area that exhibit work by local artists? Put together a contact list and start your outreach, e-mailing or calling the galleries and other spaces to inquire about their submission guidelines. Once you have these, you can decide which ones you would like to pursue. Note that it's usually easier to get into a group show than to have a gallery owner agree to give you a solo show, so you may want to start there. Diane Koss of Cutesy But Not Cutesy started by reaching out to a new gallery that had put a call for entries on Craigslist. When she responded to the ad, the gallery asked her to come in to show her work in person. She took a gamble and brought some of her monster pieces. She didn't think they would like them, but she lucked out.

The fun side of pursuing gallery work is that it allows you to be a bit more creative with your product line and to break out of the monotony of production. Feel free to push the envelope. What works for your product line may be too staid and conservative for a gallery. Diane Koss says, "Making stuff for galleries gives me a break from my normal monster production. I try to make them more conceptual even though they are still monsters. It gives me a chance to expand my brain and do something different." Even though you are stretching your creative muscles, make sure that the work you do is in line with your brand and that what you offer to a gallery still looks and feels like *your* work.

When taking photographs of your work to submit to galleries for consideration, you'll need to think more conservatively. You may be used to photographing your products in a way that works for online sales and craft fairs, but art galleries are more conservative, and the representation of your work should reflect this. Photograph your work straight on, up close. Don't submit photos of your illustrations in

> *"Making stuff for galleries gives me a break from my normal monster production."*
>
> —**DIANE KOSS** of Cutesy But Not Cutesy

frames on a wall in a room setting—show only the illustrations. The same goes for sculpture and for jewelry and other wearables. "Start to think about your work in the context of being in a white-walled space," says illustrator Lisa Congdon. The photographs should show only the artwork, without the kind of setting that would help set the piece in context for a craft buyer.

When you're accepted by a gallery, review the terms of the contract carefully, and make sure you understand what the shipping requirements are, who is responsible for the safety of your work while it's in the gallery's hands, and what the payment terms are. Average commission rates run between 30 and 50 percent for a gallery. Lisa urges a thoughtful relationship with any gallery or space you are exhibiting in. "When you are turning over your work for someone else to sell, you want to make sure you are protected." She continues, "Anything you might be worried about, get it in writing."

Don't be afraid of rejection. You will be rejected from a lot of gallery shows, but if this is an avenue you really want to pursue, don't give up. If appropriate, ask for feedback on why you were not accepted into a show. If asked nicely, curators may respond, but they're likely to give you a very frank answer, so be prepared for it. Learn from it and move on. Diane Koss, who's had her fair share of rejections, used to hang her rejection letters on the refrigerator to keep herself motivated.

Getting Work into Museums

If you can picture your work in galleries, then dreaming of seeing it in a museum isn't that far fetched. It is a goal to be encouraged, but also tempered with caution. A museum's purpose is to preserve and document history. So what makes something "museum worthy"? "Things that hold up and stand the test of time are just good objects," says Namita Gupta Wiggers, curator of the Museum of Contemporary Craft in Portland, Oregon. "Museums don't collect everything, and the fact of the matter is, out of a lot of the people that are working today, only a small handful will be put into museums to be preserved for future generations. The rest of that material is going to be preserved in people's homes and their attics and basements, and rediscovered by someone else down the road."

It is a lofty goal to want to be the representative of a movement or a generation. The best thing you can do, Namita suggests, is to "work hard and constantly try to work better. Use care with your materials and care with what you're making. Ask yourself, Why am I making what I am?"

Museum Shops

Don't want to wait around several decades before your work has a chance to be seen in a museum? There's a shortcut. Get your work into museum gift shops! No one can resist browsing through the items in a museum gift shop after spending time in a museum.

If you think your products would be a good fit for a museum gift shop, start compiling a list of museum shops you'd like to sell in. Find out if they purchase via wholesale or consignment. Smaller shops may be more open to consignment, but the larger museum shops will most likely be stocked by wholesale buyers. Check their websites, or pick up the phone to find out.

The New York and San Francisco International Gift Fairs are good trade shows to exhibit at if you want to reach this audience. But there's also a trade show specifically for museum stores: the Museum Store Association Retail Conference & Expo (museumstoreassociation.org), which takes place annually and caters specifically to museum-shop buyers and retailers. Exhibiting at this show will place you directly in the path of this particular audience.

Chapter

10

WALKING THE WALK

By deciding to pursue your creative, crafty career, you have entered the creative marketplace, a world shared by many like-minded individuals. Members of the handmade community share a lot of common values—treating yourself and your employees well, finding a better way of life, and believing in the products you make.

It's exciting when you are able to pursue your goals and dreams. It is even more exciting when you discover that there are many others who have similar visions of the community you want to be involved with. Crafters share a need to create and to make in order to live a fulfilling life. It is all about leading the life you want to lead.

Joining a Welcoming Community

By owning and running a handmade business, you become part of a vibrant community. And what a welcoming community it is—where people will envelop you with loving arms and where there's always more room at the table. As an unspoken rule, members of the handmade community will go out of their way to help one another succeed. You'll find a built-in cheerleading team full of positive energy and a willingness to share knowledge.

In the corporate world, knowledge is proprietary; in the handmade community, it's shared. Makers are more relaxed about processes and sources and contacts. Crafters want their friends to succeed, and if they see a way to help someone out, they'll try to make a connection for that person.

By adopting this pay-it-forward attitude, you'll develop meaningful personal and professional relationships. You'll share experiences with people who, just like you, are trying to make a living from their creativity. As Shauna Alterio of Something's Hiding in Here relates: "The reason we really fell in love with doing this is the community. When we did our first show, I remember sitting there thinking, 'There's all these other kids that are just like us—they love to make things,' and it was just a major eye-opening thing for us.

"We had both had a fine-arts background. And we were functioning in a really strict gallery circuit, which is not nurturing. There is no community about it at all. It is just cutthroat, and no one is in it to support each other. All of a sudden, we found ourselves surrounded by all these people who want to help you and are genuine in wanting to share their sources and to give you advice on things. We made all these really amazing connections with people who have become our closest friends now.

"Because of that circuit, whether it be other artists who are making things, or people who are running shops, or curators who are putting together shows and exhibitions, we really found a community where we fit, and this amazing network of people we respect so much. They are a constant source of inspiration."

Craft Mafias, Stitch 'n Bitch groups, Etsy Teams, and local craft groups (including groups sponsored by craft supplies stores) are all places where you can network offline—attending craft nights, socializing, and learning new skills for your craft or business. Such groups can be support networks, sounding boards, or just opportunities to get out of your house or studio. Crafting can be a solitary existence, and it's important for your sanity for you to have some social interaction.

Networking and connecting isn't confined to "real" life. The Internet has opened up the entire handmade community worldwide, and the support network flows online as well as off. If you ask a question or for an opinion online, you will get an answer. Your friends and fans will do their best to point you in the right direction. You'll be amazed at how giving people are, and how willing they are to pay it forward.

Being Your Own Best Customer

As a crafter and seller, you are part of the handmade community. But are you also supporting the community? The easiest and best way to do so is to be your own best customer *for other crafters*. It's about telling everyone you meet about your amazing new wallet from Queen Bee Creations or your adorable bunny ring from Figs & Ginger.

There is an intimate connection between buyers and crafters. When someone purchases one of the tea towels you created with your own two hands, you have a connection with that person, and the customer feels the good vibes that come from supporting a small-business owner doing something that he or she loves. Craft consumers like knowing who the maker is: They can ask all the questions they want about a product they're buying instead of relying on a label that may give only country of origin. And by understanding your process and the time and energy that go into your making, they can discover the "soul" in the products they buy.

Today, many people are purchasing higher-quality items. When the economy took a hit and extra spending money became hard to come by, customers became pickier about their purchases. They wanted products that would last. They wanted to stretch their dollars, but also to know that the money they did have was going to good use.

When you, as a maker, choose to purchase handmade items yourself, you're not only supporting other artists but also investing in high-quality items that have a history, a story that brings meaning into your world. There's an ethic within the handmade community that says that by supporting one another, you are supporting the idea that crafters can make a living from their work—and isn't that what you yourself are striving for? If you are asking your customers to support you by purchasing your work, you should turn around and do the same thing.

When you have a good sale or show, reinvest some of that money back into the community of other crafters and makers. This can help the handmade economy grow. The more dollars that are spent on handmade goods, the more handmade goods there will be for sale. Your crafter friends may offer you deals, and it's fine to accept such discounts, but it's also fine to let them know they are worth it by paying the full price.

Kari Chapin, author of *The Handmade Marketplace* has a "buy handmade" rule: "If I can buy something handmade for the same price, like a handbag that's going to be sixty dollars on Etsy or at a craft show or sixty dollars at Macy's, then I choose to go with the handmade version," she says.

It's a matter of principal. If you chose to be a part of the handmade community but are not purchasing handmade items from your peers, you're missing out not only on some quality products but also on the larger point of the community.

Earning Green Cred

If you want to walk the walk and talk the talk, there are other things you can do besides purchasing goods and services from the handmade community. You can, for example, go green.

Many crafters label themselves "green," meaning that they pursue environmentally friendly business practices. In one way, this is an easy switch to flip. Just by being a small business, you are much more environmentally sound than a large corporation. But there is a lot you can do to become more environmentally aware about how you conduct business.

There are several resources on how to run a green business, such as the *Green Business Guide* from the Small Business Administration. Reduce, reuse, and recycle when you can. Many crafters use recycled, upcycled, thrifted, and vintage materials in the products they create, as well as in their craft fair setups, in their packaging, and around the studio.

Sara Selepouchin of Girls Can Tell believes everyone has "a responsibility to make their footprint as small as possible." She continues: "It's definitely how I live, and I imagine my customers want to minimize their footprint to some degree. I like to focus on things in my line that are reusable versus disposable—things like lunch bags, towels, and coasters. It's important to love what you have and want to keep it for a while."

A friend of Rhonda and Elijah Wyman, of Figs & Ginger, enlightened them on the plight of Mother Nature and how they could do something about it, even in their jewelry-making business. They started small by printing their postcards with an environmentally friendly printing service. Then they installed solar panels on their trailer. And then they really got down to business. Rhonda explains, "I was getting a lot of headaches, so I started looking into alternatives to the chemicals we used in the studio, and I searched out how to make your own pickle [a type of acid used to clean soldered jewelry]. We did a lot of experimenting to find the right things we needed. At that time no one was selling recycled metal, and we were having to get it refined ourselves. Then Hoover & Strong started selling recycled metals, and that was really helpful. They don't do any new mining at all. They offer a lot of information about mining. Silver mining is so unregulated, I realized how the earth is being destroyed so I can make jewelry, and I thought, 'Okay, I'm kind of a jerk.' We decided no new mining for our company, although it ended up having to be 'as little new mining as possible,' as it's impossible to be one hundred percent sure."

While it may seem impossible to change an industry such as mining, Rhonda and Elijah found a way to feel comfortable with their business. All it takes is some research and creativity to find materials that you feel comfortable with as a crafter and that you can pass along to your customers, knowing that those materials won't harm them or the environment.

Helping Out

Beyond the general camaraderie and mutual supportiveness that prevail in the indie craft community, there's another trait that community members share: a willingness to help out during a crisis. Rhonda and Elijah Wyman learned of the community's capacity to help during a very scary time in their lives. Elijah had come down with a kidney disease that was killing him.

He had to get a transplant. Because Elijah could no longer work, Rhonda was working eighty- to ninety-hour weeks, doing a nannying job as well as making jewelry.

"The indie scene really pulled through for us," Rhonda says. "They were doing charities and donations. It was just amazing the way the community supported us through that time."

Because so many crafters have to forgo health insurance, it's become fairly typical for community members to pool their money to help out people in need. It is a "we're all in this together" mentality that exemplifies how caring the indie crowd can be.

And when the devastating earthquakes hit Haiti in 2010 and then Japan in 2011, crafters pulled together fundraisers and auctions for earthquake relief. Special-edition prints, T-shirts, and various other products were designed and made to entice buyers to give to relief efforts.

Individual online shops were donating 10 percent of sales, and blogs such as *Indie Fixx* were organizing auctions where all goods were donated and all proceeds went to relief efforts.

Dealing with "the F Word"

A crafter is someone who loves to create and loves to problem-solve. Someone who is ambitious and tenacious. Someone who has the drive and willingness to go after what he or she wants and to put in the hard work to make it happen. But there can be a lot of missteps along the way.

We have been trained from an early age that failure is a bad thing and that it should be avoided. But in reality you *will* make mistakes and things *will* get screwed up. You'll look back and wonder "What was I thinking?" But failure is a part of the learning process. Every time you make a mistake, every time you screw something up, every time you utterly fail, you ultimately come away that much smarter.

Your failures need to be acknowledged and celebrated, right alongside your successes. In Jo Waterhouse's book *Indie Craft*, contributor Diem Chan says this about failure: "Experimenting and giving yourself permission to fail is a must in learning."

Bettie Newell of Portland, Oregon, started a craft blog, *Handmade in Portland*, that focused on the crafty happenings in the city. She took on two partners because she knew it wasn't something she could do on her own. The site experienced some growing pains. The community was supportive, but the bloggers had trouble figuring out their editorial content. "By the end of that year, it was clear the partnership wasn't going to work out. So we decided to part ways," Bettie explains. "My plan was to take *Handmade in Portland* and continue on with it. But in 2011, moving forward, I realized that wasn't realistic. I couldn't do a website like that on my own. It wasn't really how I wanted to spend my time. So I decided to let it go, which was sad, but the right decision."

Clearly a hard lesson to learn, but Bettie survived and now blogs at *Little Paper Cities*. She took a chance and had

How Big Is Too Big?

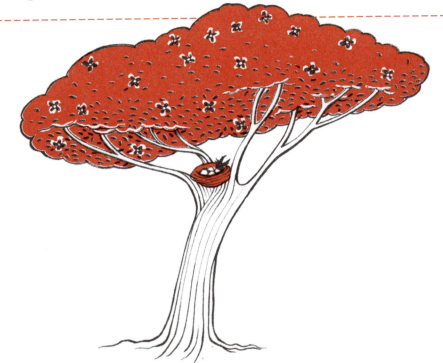

You need to have a clear idea of how big you want to become. It's natural to want to expand your business, but is bigger always better? Will becoming bigger mean losing your handmade focus?

There may come a time when you are faced with the decision whether to outsource your production overseas or to license your work to a large corporation. If you make such a move, you may not be able to call yourself a handmade business anymore.

You may feel pressure to keep scaling up and growing and producing more profit. You may feel that it's something that you *have* to do. But in reality it isn't. You can choose the size of the business you want. You can choose to stay small. You don't have to take a handmade business and turn it over to a faceless company selling overexposed goods.

Tina Seamonster had been fulfilling wholesale orders of her zombie bookmarks for Books-A-Million when they asked her if she could also create magnets. Not one to turn down an opportunity, Tina said, "Of course, I can do it." Books-A-Million wanted rectangular magnets with a Mylar coating. As she researched outsourcing the manufacturing of the magnets, Tina found a reasonably priced option in the United States, but she didn't like the company's politics. She then researched production options in China, but she ultimately decided against it because she felt as though she wasn't dealing with a real person, plus the shipping from China to the United States was outrageously expensive. In the end, she purchased her own magnet-making machine and all the magnet parts and became her own production line, pumping out 4,875 magnets for the initial Books-A-Million order. "Between magnets and bookmarks, I've delivered over 35,000 pieces in about a year all on my own," she says, and by doing the work herself, she still comes out ahead in terms of profit.

Overexposure is something that Ryan and Lucy Berkley of Berkley Illustration struggle with. Ryan says, "I have this thing in my head where I don't want my prints to be completely overexposed." They've had offers from Target and Nordstrom to license their images for T-shirts, but they've turned those opportunities down. Says Ryan, "It's just something in my mind that told me that I didn't really want to oversaturate my artwork to where I'm afraid that one day I'll just be burnt out and people just won't be interested anymore."

Sarah and Victor Lytvinenko think about the growth of their company, Raleigh Denim, a lot, but right now they're happy with the size they are. For independent crafters, they're pretty big, but they look small in the context of the larger jeans market. Whereas big denim production facilities with automated machines make about 12,000 pairs a day (one pair every twelve minutes), Sarah and Victor produce about 150 pairs of jeans per week, completing one pair every few hours. Yes, their company *could* grow a bit more, but as Sarah says, "How can we grow without selling out and being too huge and losing the sort of the soul and human touch that we've got?" They do have a stopgap in place: Sarah and Victor still sign every pair of jeans they make, and when they get to the point where they are no longer able to do that, they'll know they've stretched far enough.

You just can't compare yourself to the big-box stores. What you're doing is reeducating people about where and how the goods they buy are created—letting them know that there is a person on the other end of the line, cutting fabric and making jeans, putting together magnets, screenprinting T-shirts. You're helping them relearn what handmade really is.

the guts to screw up. If you don't take chances, you'll never find success. The phrase "big risks bring big rewards" is quite apt. As Mark Frauenfelder writes in his book *Made by Hand: Searching for Meaning in a Throwaway World* (New York: Portfolio, 2010), "Mistakes are a sign that you're active and curious."

Making mistakes means you are changing and growing as a crafter, and successful crafters are not defeated by failure. They use failure as a learning experience that will make their business all that much better. They can pick themselves up off the floor and step back into the fray with even more vim and vigor.

Keeping Your Sanity

"Sustainability" doesn't just mean causing less harm to the environment. It also means being able to sustain the level of business you want while maintaining your health and sanity.

With their do-it-yourself mentality, crafters who have a handmade business often find it hard to give up control over any part of that business. You get it in your head that you can do everything yourself. This creation is yours, so why would you give control over anything to someone else?

But there comes a time when that DIY attitude isn't sustainable or advisable. "I think the switch comes with scale," says Sarah Lytvinenko of Raleigh Denim. "You can do everything if you're making fifteen hats, and you're handling the orders from three different callers and searching for one type of yarn. You can do that. But when that triples, can you do all of that as well as the branding, as well as the PR, as well as remembering what account the money goes in, as well as the taxes, as well as the labeling and packaging? I think the answer is lots of people can do it, but can you do it for a long period of time? If you're trying to build a business, then you need to be sustainable."

One day you are going to need a vacation. What happens then? Sarah continues,

"I have learned that there are parts I need to let go." But that's a hard lesson for many crafters to learn.

So take care of yourself. Do what you need to do to run a well-balanced crafty business, but don't expect to have to do everything. Listen to what your body is telling you, and, bit by bit, give some control to those you trust. Because when you do, you'll have more time to do the things you really love, thinking up the next big thing instead of worrying about the taxes or the pattern cutting. It will help you get back to why you got involved in this business in the first place—all those reasons that often get lost in the shuffle of running the day-to-day.

Remember you are a person and not a machine. That's part of the very definition of handmade.

RESOURCES

Crafty People

Shauna Alterio and Stephen Loidolt
Something's Hiding in Here
Philadelphia, PA
somethingshidinginhere.com

Ryan and Lucy Berkley
Berkley Illustration
Portland, OR
etsy.com/shop/
berkleyillustration

Lisa Congdon
San Francisco, CA
lisacongdon.com

Jena Coray
Miss Modish
Portland, OR
missmodish.com

Alison Dryer
Pistol Stitch Designs
Baltimore, MD
pistol-stitched.com

Sue Eggen
Giant Dwarf
Philadelphia, PA
giantdwarfdesign.blogspot.
com

Jeffrey Everett
El Jefe Design
Washington, DC
eljefedesign.com

Kasey and Kelly Evick
Biggs and Featherbelle
Baltimore, MD
biggsandfeather.com

Diane Gilleland
Crafty Pod
craftypod.com

Jenny Hart
Sublime Stitching
Austin, TX
sublimestitching.com

Ben High
Los Angeles, CA
benhigh.com

Garth Johnson
Extreme Craft
extremecraft.com

Diane Koss
Cutesy But Not Cutesy
Philadelphia, PA
etsy.com/shop/dkoss2

Sarah and Victor Lytvinenko
Raleigh Denim
Raleigh, NC
raleighworkshop.com

Danielle Maveal
Etsy's Seller Education
Coordinator
Brooklyn, NY
etsy.com

Lee Meredith
Leethal
Portland, OR
leethal.net

Bettie Newell
Little Paper Cities
Portland, OR
littlepapercities.com

Willo O'Brien
WilloToons
San Francisco, CA
willotoons.com

Rebecca Pearcy
Queen Bee Creations
Portland, OR
queenbee-creations.com

Paul Roden and Valerie Lueth
Tugboat Printshop
Pittsburgh, PA
tugboatprintshop.com

Tina Seamonster
Washington, DC
etsy.com/shop/
tinaseamonster

Sara Selepouchin
Girls Can Tell
Philadelphia, PA
girlscantell.com

Becky Striepe
Glue and Glitter
Atlanta, GA
glueandglitter.com

Namita Gupta Wiggers
Curator
Museum of Contemporary
Craft, in partnership
with Pacific Northwest
College of Art
museumofcontemporarycraft.
org
pnca.edu

Jon Wye
Washington, DC
jonwye.com

Elijah and Rhonda Wyman
Figs & Ginger
Asheville, NC
figsandginger.com

Online Marketplaces

ArtFire
artfire.com

Big Cartel
bigcartel.com

Buyolympia
buyolympia.com

Cosa Verde
cosaverde.com

Craftland
craftlandshow.com

Etsy
etsy.com

Renegade Handmade
renegadehandmade.com

Shana Logic
shanalogic.com

Shopify
shopify.com

Storenvy
storenvy.com

Supermarket
supermarkethq.com

Trunkt
trunkt.com

Zen Cart
zen-cart.com

Craft Fairs

Art Star Craft Bazaar
Philadelphia, PA
artstarcraftbazaar.com

Art vs. Craft
Milwaukee, WI
artvscraftmke.blogspot.com

Bazaar Bizarre
Boston, MA; Cleveland, OH;
San Francisco, CA; San
Mateo, CA (Maker Faire)
bazaarbizarre.org

***Bust* Craftacular**
New York, NY
bust.com/craftacular/
craftacular-home.html

**Crafty Bastards Arts &
Crafts Fair**
Washington, DC
washingtoncitypaper.com/
craftybastards

Crafty Wonderland
Portland, OR
craftywonderland.com

Indie Craft Experience
Atlanta, GA
ice-atlanta.com

Renegade Craft Fairs
Austin, TX; Brooklyn, NY; San
Francisco, CA; Los Angeles,
CA; Chicago, IL; London,
England
renegadecraft.com

Urban Craft Uprising
Seattle, WA
urbancraftuprising.com

Brick-and-Mortar Shops

Arizona
Made Art Boutique
922 North Fifth Street
Phoenix, AZ 85004
madephx.com

California
Rare Device
1845 Market Street
San Francisco, CA 94103
raredevice.net

Urban Fauna Studio
1315 16th Avenue
San Francisco, CA 94122
urbanfaunastudio.com

Wallflower Boutique
103 Locust Street
Santa Cruz, CA 95060
shopthewallflower.com

Colorado
Fancy Tiger Crafts / Fancy Tiger Clothing
1 South Broadway
Denver, CO 80209
fancytiger.com

Georgia
Young Blood Gallery & Boutique
636 North Highland Avenue
Atlanta, GA 30306
youngbloodgallery.com

Iowa
Domestica
321 East Walnut Street
Des Moines, IA 50309
shopdomestica.com

Maryland
Double Dutch Boutique
3616 Falls Road
Baltimore, MD 21211
doubledutchboutique.com

Trohv
921 West 36th Street
Baltimore, MD 21211
trohvshop.com

Massachusetts
Magpie
416 Highland Avenue
Somerville, MA 02144
magpie-store.com

Minnesota
Bad Cat Creations
315 Irvine Avenue, NW
Bemidji, MN 56601
badcatcreations.com

New York
Greenwich Letterpress
39 Christopher Street
New York, NY 10014
greenwichletterpress.com

Space Craft Brooklyn
355 Bedford Avenue
Brooklyn, NY 11211
spacecraftbrooklyn.com

North Carolina
Epona & Oak
329 Blake Street
Raleigh, NC 27601
eponaandoak.com

Ohio
Fabricate
4037 Hamilton Avenue
Cincinnati, OH 45223
fabnorthside.com

Wholly Craft
3169 North High Street
Columbus, OH 43202
whollycraft.net

Oregon
Frock
1439 NE Alberta Street
Portland, OR 97211
frockboutique.com

Land
3925 North Mississippi Avenue
Portland, OR 97227
buyolympia.com

Pennsylvania
Art Star
623 North 2nd Street
Philadelphia, PA 19123
artstarphilly.com

Pterodactyl
3237 Amber Street
Philadelphia, PA 19134
pterodactylphiladelphia.org

Rhode Island
Craftland
235 Westminster Street
Providence, RI 02903
craftlandshow.com

Texas
Make Shop & Studio
313 North Bishop Avenue
Dallas, TX 75208
themakesite.com

The WonderCraft
1601 East Cesar Chavez
Austin, TX 78702
thewondercraft.com

Virginia
Fibre Space
102 North Fayette Street
Alexandria, VA 22314
fibrespace.com

Washington, DC
Nana
3068 Mount Pleasant Street
NW
Washington, DC 20009
nanadc.com

Smash Records
2314 18th Street NW
Washington, DC 20009
smashrecords.com

Trohv
232 Carroll Street NW
Washington, DC 20012
trohvshop.com

Washington State
Schmancy Toys
1932 2nd Avenue
Seattle, WA 98101
schmancytoys.com

Wisconsin
Zip-Dang
2606 Monroe Street
Madison, WI 53711
zip-dang.com

Trade Shows

ACRE
Las Vegas, NV
acrelasvegas.com

American Craft Council
Baltimore, MD
craftcouncil.org

Buyers Market of American Craft
Baltimore, MD
buyersmarketof
americancraft.com

CHA Conference and Trade Show
craftandhobby.org

Museum Store Association Retail Conference & Expo
museumstore
association.org

National Stationery Show
New York, NY
nationalstationeryshow.com

New York International Gift Fair
New York, NY
nyigf.com

One of a Kind Show and Sale
Chicago, IL
oneofakindshow.com

Pool Tradeshow
Las Vegas, NV
pooltradeshow.com

San Francisco International Gift Fair
San Francisco, CA
sfigf.com

SOFA
Santa Fe, NM; Chicago, IL; New York, NY
sofaexpo.com

Surtex
New York, NY
surtex.com

Craft Schools

Arrowmont School of Arts and Crafts
Gatlinburg, TN
arrowmont.org

Haystack Mountain School of Crafts
Deer Isle, ME
haystack-mtn.org

Penland School of Crafts
Penland, NC
penland.org

INDEX

HELLO CRAFT offers yearly memberships to crafters and makers of all levels and interests. Our members enjoy discounts on Hello Craft events and receive marketing tips and tools for successful branding and selling. Becoming a Hello Craft member connects you to a larger network of crafters who share a commitment to the handmade community.

As a special thank-you for purchasing our awesome book, we'd like to offer you a yearlong Hello Craft membership for half off! Hooray!

With a Hello Craft membership you receive

- Admission to Hello Craft events at a special registration rate
- Exclusive e-newsletters
- Access to members-only sections of the website
- Members' welcome e-mail
- A membership web graphic for your site
- A birthday surprise

And you get the knowledge that you're helping to support the hand-made community!

As an extra-special thank-you, Hello Craft members have access to original resources used in researching this book, including links, blog posts, images, videos, and audio interviews with the lovely people quoted in *Handmade to Sell*!

To take advantage of this offer, go to hellocraft.com/book.

Thanks for reading.
xoxo
Hello Craft loves you!